The Project Manager's Guide to Health Information Technology Implementation

Susan M. Houston, MBA, RN-BC, PMP, CPHIMS

HIMSS Mission

To lead healthcare transformation through effective use of health information technology.

About the Author

Susan M. Houston, MBA, RN-BC, PMP, CPHIMS, has extensive clinical, nurse informatics and project management experience. She has used project management principles to successfully manage and complete both large and small projects. Ms. Houston has certifications in Nursing Informatics from AANC; Project Management Professional from PMI; and Certified Professional in Healthcare Information and Management Systems from HIMSS. Her formal education includes a Bachelor of Science in Nursing and a Masters of Business Administration.

Ms. Houston started working in an emergency room while in nursing school. After graduation, she continued to work in emergency medicine for more than 15 years, finishing as a nurse manager of a Level 2 trauma center. Ms. Houston was then asked to implement a clinical information system because she was one of the few nurses who were comfortable with computers. This began her career as a project manager implementing clinical systems. She has worked for a software vendor and as a consultant implementing a wide range of applications and processes for a variety of healthcare organizations.

She spent a number of years on the board of directors for the Project Management Institute's Healthcare Special Interest Group, which was recently converted to the Healthcare Community of Practice. Ms. Houston was also on the faculty at the University of Maryland Baltimore School of Nursing where she taught Information Technology Project Management for the Master's of Nursing Informatics program. Ms. Houston has presented at a number of local and national conferences, as well as co-authored a number of articles and the book *Project Management for Healthcare Informatics*. She has authored a number of courses in the HIMSS eLearning Academy.

Ms. Houston currently works at the National Institutes of Health, Clinical Center. While at the Clinical Center, she developed a Project Management Office that is responsible for managing multiple large and small projects while mentoring other project managers throughout the hospital. Ms. Houston is the Chief of Portfolio Management, responsible for the implementation and configuration management of the clinical and administrative applications used in the Clinical Center. This includes a variety of commercially and custom-developed systems used by one or more departments or throughout the hospital.

Contents

Preface

Susan M. Houston, MBA, RN-BC, PMP, CPHIMS

We are heading in the direction of a paperless healthcare system. Some feel we will never be completely paperless, while others are more optimistic. Either way, we are in the middle of an invasion of information technology in the healthcare industry. With this comes the need for project management and the understanding of what it takes to implement software. Some software projects are large, multi-year efforts to bring a full electronic health record to an organization, while others are smaller niche systems for a few users. Some will be purchased from a company that developed the software for sale, while others will be built just for a single, unique need.

It is important for project managers to have a toolkit where they can draw upon tools and concepts for each project they manage. Since each project is unique, the necessary tools will vary from one to the other. One primary tool every project manager should have is *A Guide to the Project Management Body of Knowledge (PMBOK®)* by the Project Management Institute.

As project managers move through each project, they will gather more tools to add to their toolbox to be used in future projects. This book provides essential concepts for any project manager who will be leading a project to implement health information technology. The early chapters will provide a review for experienced project managers, as well as an introduction for those new to the industry. The later chapters introduce concepts and define terms used for software implementation projects that will add more tools for use in HIT projects.

A project manager is rarely an expert in the design, development, testing, training or technical implementation of software, and this should not be the expectation. This book provides an overview of software and hardware concepts that will allow the project manager to understand aspects of implementation projects. It would be difficult to provide a complete guide to project management, software development, hardware configuration and how to implement each. This book will not make you an expert in these areas, but it will provide guidance so the right questions are asked of those who are the experts.

Acknowledgments

I would like to thank everyone who supported me during the writing of this book, especially my husband Gary, who seems to have an unlimited supply of patience and encouragement. To my children, Nicole and Matt, thank you for your ongoing support and sense of humor.

A word of thanks to Nix, at Infinity Plus One Studio for the wonderful graphics used throughout the book.

And finally, a special thank you to Patty, Tim and Yulia for their time and guidance. Your friendship and support are always appreciated.

—Susan M. Houston

CHAPTER 1

What Is a Project?

"Management is doing things right; leadership is doing the right things."
—*Peter F. Drucker*

The healthcare industry is going through a significant change: the conversion from paper to electronic health records (EHR). To facilitate this change, the federal government has programs in place to encourage adoption. This effort began with President George W. Bush's call for all Americans to have an EHR by 2014, and continued with President Barack Obama's funding through the American Recovery and Reinvestment Act (ARRA) of 2009, specifically the Health Information Technology for Economic and Clinical Health (HITECH) Act. These changes prompted an increased interest in project management within the healthcare industry in anticipation of the expected explosion in clinical software implementation.

There are many types of software. However, this book will focus only on two broad categories: **commercial off-the-shelf** (COTS) and **custom developed**. Although both kinds of software are implemented using the same project management processes, some of the activities that occur along the way are different.

Software vendors develop COTS systems with the intention of selling them to a range of customers whose organizational size and structure and whose specific needs, results and workflow can vary enormously. To accommodate the diversity of their customer base, COTS are often generic in design and highly configurable, allowing customers to make modifications to fit unique workflows. The amount of work needed to customize COTS software varies among systems and should not be viewed as a minor task.

Custom-developed software, on the other hand, is developed with a single organization or use in mind. This software is based on specific requirements to fit a specific need. The development can be done internally or can be contracted out to a software development company. The similarities and differences between these two projects will be reviewed throughout this book.

Basic project management concepts are reviewed in Chapter 2 through Chapter 4. While these chapters do not provide an in-depth study of project management, they will provide a review for experienced project managers, as well as an introduction for those new to the role.

The next chapters outline topics related to implementing software, and include terminology and concepts that project managers will find useful during implementation of their first software project. While project managers are not expected to be **subject-matter experts** (SME), if they understand the basic concepts and terminology, they will be better prepared to ask the right questions and ensure the best decisions are made based on discussions with the project team. Key concepts, such as testing options, configuration and change management, planning for activation and post-live support are also reviewed.

Two case studies will span the book, allowing readers to apply concepts described in each chapter. All software projects are different. There are no right or wrong answers, but some choices are better than others. The project management methodology you adopt needs to be flexible and adaptable in order to fit the needs and complexity of the project and its organization.

> Two case studies will be provided at the end of each chapter; additional information will be provided, along with questions related to the chapter. At the end of the book, a brief response will be provided for each question. Please remember, each situation is unique, and there is no wrong answer. It is perfectly acceptable if your answer does not match the author's.

A Guide to the Project Management Body of Knowledge (*PMBOK*®), published by the Project Management Institute (PMI), provides a framework of best practices for project management practitioners. *PMBOK*® should be part of every project manager's toolkit as they adopt their methodology to fit the size and complexity of the project and the culture of the organization. This book follows *PMBOK*®, but provides additional insights for implementing software specific to healthcare.

> • A project manager is not expected to be a subject-matter expert.
> • Each stakeholder brings a unique viewpoint to the project.

WHAT IS A PROJECT?

Understanding the definition of a **project** is an important first step in understanding project management. A project is a temporary activity that becomes progressively elaborated as you move through the lifecycle, and produces a unique **product**, **service**, or **result**. Because of these characteristics, a project is different from a process. Implementing a new software system is a project, but so are some activities undertaken during the operations and maintenance of the same system, such as upgrading the hardware or software.

Because it is a temporary endeavor, a project has a defined beginning and end. A project begins when a need is identified and ends when the specific objectives are achieved and are formally accepted by the sponsor. A project also can end if a decision is made to terminate prior to achieving the final outcome. This decision can be made for a number of reasons, such as determining that the objectives cannot be met, the need no longer exists or resources are no longer available. Organizations should define what criteria are important for evaluating when to terminate a project.

The temporary nature of a project does not relate specifically to the project's duration. Projects can last weeks or years, but every project goes through all phases of the project lifecycle. The time spent in each phase will vary based on the amount of work required.

As projects are temporary endeavors, the project team is usually also temporary. Team members often work together for the purpose of the specific project only, and once the project ends, are released to return to other work or projects. A critical consideration for the project manager is that the members may not have worked together in the past. A focus on getting them to work as a team should begin as early as possible once the team has been assembled. This is often accomplished through offsite social or team-building activities.

A project is developed in steps and continues in increments. Work is coordinated and detailed through a specific plan that is defined early and updated as more information is obtained. The plan includes a set of related tasks that are modified or expanded as the project progresses. Development begins with the broad scope and becomes more elaborate as functional requirements are defined; this is then followed by system design. The requirements and design are needed to help define the test phase, and the development feeds decisions around what to include in the training materials. This process is very controlled and known during project planning. It is important to note that this elaboration is not the same as the uncontrolled aspect of **scope creep**. Figure 1-1 shows how a project can become more defined as the layers are peeled and more details are identified.

Figure 1-1: The Many Layers of a Project. (From Houston S: Project Manager's Guide to Healthcare Informatics. HIMSS eLearning Academy. 2009.)

A project produces a defined outcome, such as a unique **product**, **service** or **result**. This final deliverable is what provides the guideline for when the project is considered complete. As mentioned earlier, if it becomes apparent that the outcomes cannot be reached, the project should be terminated. Defining outcomes early in the project lifecycle also provides direction and boundaries for the rest of the project.

A **product** is a defined deliverable, such as new software to track the menus and diet orders for patients along with the ability to track the ordering and management of food supplies. In every case, a project comprises all of the work to create and deliver a unique product, as depicted in Figure 1-2.

A **service** is a deliverable that is less tangible than a product, but supports a defined business function. Developing a new training program or workflow for patient transfers are examples of service-focused projects. It is important to note that the project is to *develop* or *set-up* the service, not the ongoing effort of providing the service.

A project can also produce a specific **result**. Conducting research produces a specific result. The presence of repeating elements, such as data collection, does not change the uniqueness of a project. The project begins with background research and a documented hypothesis and ends with the documented conclusion (i.e., a published article or presentation). In most cases, the conclusion, or increased knowledge, is the specific result that defines the end of the project. If this conclusion leads to further research, a new project would begin.

Figure 1-2: Projects Comprise All of the Work to Create and Deliver a Unique Product. (From Houston S: Project Manager's Guide to Healthcare Informatics. HIMSS eLearning Academy. 2009.)

PROJECT MANAGEMENT

A highly clarifying question to ask right away is whether **project management**, **program management** and **portfolio management** are the same thing or different. Project management will be defined here, while program management and portfolio management will be defined in the next chapter.

Project management is the application of knowledge, skills, tools and techniques to project activities to meet project requirements, according to *PMBOK®*.

It is accomplished through the application and integration of project management processes, which will be defined in Chapter 3. There also are areas of knowledge that help define the management processes required to successfully complete a project. These knowledge areas will be further defined in Chapter 4.

Ultimately, project management is a framework that defines how a project will be managed, and the project manager, by guiding each step of the framework, is responsible for the success or failure of the project.

Based on the definition of a project provided earlier, project management differs from general management in a number of ways. The project team is brought together to complete a defined set of activities within a defined timeline. This demands that the project manager be able to build the team to work together within a finite period of time. This will invariably include what some call "micro-management." The project manager needs to know when each task is completed, of any potential delays and any issues or risks that might arise. Tracking this information is critical because of the possibility of rapid change within projects to which the project manager must be able to quickly adapt the plan to keep the project on time. A general manager, on the other hand, manages by exception; staff follows standard policies and procedures to complete their routine work.

A project manager must be able to focus on the daily details to ensure that the project stays on schedule while keeping an eye on the larger picture, to be proactive about how today's activities might impact tomorrow and plan accordingly. The need to conform tasks to deadlines and deliverables is more pronounced in project management than in general management. This precision in conforming tasks to deadlines and deliverables is more pronounced in project management than in general management.

Having a person with the right skill set in the project manager role is critical to success. Often individuals are placed in this role because they understand the business processes or they have the time to take on the project. However, if an individual does not have the right skills, he or she is simply being set up to fail. A good project manager must be able to lead the team and facilitate the completion of tasks or activities, all while communicating down to the team and up to the sponsors and organizational leadership.

In terms of the necessary skill set, although some feel subject matter knowledge is necessary, the project manager is not expected to be an SME. Project managers should be able to manage any project if he or she has the right people on the team. With that said, it is often easier to understand the work being completed and to gain support from the team when the project manager has some knowledge related to the project.

Leadership	Facilitation
Communication	Collaboration
Critical Thinking	Analytical Thinking
Negotiation	Motivation
Decision Making	Time Management
Interpersonal Skills	Project Management Process
Flexibility	Team Management
General Management	Organization

Table 1-1: Key Skills for a Project Manager.

In the case of this book the project manager should have a basic understanding of IT, software development and healthcare. Table 1-1 illustrates some of the key skills of a project manager. Can you think of any others?

Project Stakeholders

Stakeholders are those who are actively involved or impacted by the project being undertaken. They can be project team members, sponsors or others who exert influence on the project's deliverables or team. Stakeholders can be impacted positively or negatively by the project. Stakeholders may find their staff reassigned to the project, a change to their workflow or improved access to data. The project management team should identify all stakeholders early in the project to properly evaluate their needs and expectations, since each stakeholder has a unique perspective on the project. This stakeholder analysis (see Table 1-2) also should be reviewed throughout the project, as it can change over the course of the project lifecycle.

Stakeholders can come from throughout the organization or even from outside the organization. Following are some potential stakeholders within healthcare:

- Executive Leadership. The focus of this group is often related to how the project will meet the organization's strategic mission and goals within the available budget.
- Project Sponsors. The project may have one or more sponsors. For example, an IT project might have a technical sponsor, such as the CIO, and a business sponsor, such as the head of the department who will use the new system. Sponsors often have a high level of decision-making authority within the scope of the project. Their level of authority includes approval of the scope, any requested changes and acceptance of the final deliverable at the end of the project.

Stakeholder	Involvement/ Interest in Project	Level of Influence	Level of Impact	Decision-making Authority	Expectations	Plan for Managing Expectations	Level of Support	Plan for Enhancing Support

Table 1-2: Project Stakeholder Analysis.

- End Users. Members of this group will vary between projects. When implementing computerized practitioner order entry (CPOE), for example, this group would include physicians who will enter the orders; nurses who may be able to enter phone orders; unit clerks who used to transcribe handwritten orders; and all departments who formerly received patient orders that were sent to them manually and will now receive them via the electronic system. The focus of this group is the usability of the system. Usability can include features, ease of use and even system performance.
- Vendors. Members of this group include any outside organizations that are involved in the project. This can include the vendor providing the COTS application; the vendor contracted to develop a custom application; or the consulting company providing supplemental staffing. The vendor of a legacy system that is being replaced also would be a stakeholder, since you may not have a relationship with them once their system is turned off and no longer in use.
- Project Manager. This is a very challenging and high-profile role that is often completely accountable for the success of the project. Because project managers facilitate the stakeholder analysis, they often do not think of themselves as stakeholders.
- Project Team. Each member of the project team has a stake in the project and has influence on how successful it will be. They may be fully dedicated to working on the project or they might need to balance work on the project against their regular job duties. The latter is seen more frequently, wherein the team member must balance supporting other systems with implementing a new one.
- Functional/Department Managers. These stakeholders are often focused on how the project will impact their department and their staff. The end users may report to them, or they might be end users themselves. Their department might be impacted though workflow changes, data flow changes or having their staff pulled from normal work to help with the project.

As discussed, the stakeholder analysis begins with identification of all project stakeholders. Once identified, stakeholders are evaluated for attitude toward the project, their level of influence, how the project will impact them, their decision-making authority and any barriers they might exert on the project. Each project can produce positive and negative impacts on stakeholders, as has been identified. It is important to have a plan for managing *all* stakeholders. The project manager should have a plan for how expectations will be managed, along with the best method of obtaining or enhancing support from each stakeholder. The outcome of the stakeholder analysis is often used in developing the communication management plan to ensure that the right communication is provided at the right time in the right format.

CHAPTER 2

Project, Program & Portfolio Management

"If you always blame others for your mistakes, you will never improve."

—*Joy Gumz*

The previous chapter defined project management. This chapter will define **program management** and **portfolio management**. Calling out the characteristics of each type of management in contrast to the others has great utility in helping to define particular functions. While there are some similarities between the three, there are some distinctive differences. Before these are introduced, the difference between a project and operations will be defined.

PROJECT VS. OPERATIONS

Operations and **maintenance** are often thought of as ongoing processes. Projects are not ongoing efforts, but there are activities that occur during operations and maintenance that can be considered projects if they meet the definition provided in Chapter 1. The activity of replacing hardware, upgrading the operating system and implementing software updates may all be considered projects. The activity of defining a **standard operating procedure** (SOP) also can be considered a project.

To further contrast a project to operations, in context of its layers of functions, a project is a unique, one-time undertaking—even if it is to set up a process or procedure that will be used frequently in ongoing efforts, such as those of operations, which include ongoing processes that are continuous or repeatable efforts.

Projects are managed to time, budget and quality or performance, while operations are managed to compliance and continuous improvement. The project resources' assignments are temporary, whereas operations are continuous, ongoing assignments.

There are some shared characteristics: both are performed by people, constrained by limited resources and are planned, executed and controlled. The differences are: operations are ongoing and repetitive, while projects are temporary and unique. Operations try to sustain a business and at times adopt new sets of objectives as work continues, while projects obtain an objective, then terminate.

Projects differ in size, scope and complexity. A project management methodology should be flexible enough to be tailored to the needs of the project. Guidelines should be in place to adapt the methodology to large or small projects, along with the minimum requirements.

Implementing software follows the same concept. In this, each project will be different, and so, there is no single right or wrong answer for how to implement software. The concepts reviewed in this book are intended to provide a guide for the project manager to understand terminology and concepts, not to provide the level of detail required to make the reader an SME. It is also important to note that terminology within healthcare and IT is not always clear or consistent. Each organization may utilize different terms for the same concepts, so it is highly recommended that you understand how terms are used in your organization.

PROGRAM AND PORTFOLIO MANAGEMENT

A program is a group of interrelated projects managed in a coordinated way, or a single large project broken down into individual subprojects. Projects are managed within a program when the outcomes are dependent on each other, and it is therefore prudent to manage them together.

Typically, there is a combined, common benefit, and managing them together provides control over the predecessors, risks and resources that managing separately does not provide. A program also includes elements required to manage the program, such as the methodology and infrastructure.

Tip

- Project Management ensures the projects are completed right.
- Program Management ensures the right coordination between related projects.
- Portfolio Management ensures the right projects are being done and at the right time.

Program management is the coordinated management of a program to realize its strategic objectives. This is accomplished by integrating the cost, schedule and effort of multiple projects. A project manager is assigned to each project to manage the day-to-day work, while the program manager focuses on the interdependencies between the projects.

Program managers deal with resource constraints and risks at a program level to ensure that what happens with one project does not negatively impact another or the program as a whole. The program manager coordinates the work between projects, but does not manage the individual projects.

Not all projects within the program start or end at the same time or even have the same durations. Some programs deliver benefits all at once, while others deliver benefits incrementally. This aspect would depend on the uniqueness of the program, as well as the implementation strategy.

For a program to implement an EHR with CPOE and clinical documentation, the benefits would be realized at the end of the project if the implementation strategy calls for all functionality to go-live at once, referred to as a Big Bang implementation. If the implementation strategy were to bring the functionality live in phases, such as CPOE followed by clinical documentation, the benefits would be realized on an incremental basis. It is the program manager who ensures that each go-live integrates with the systems, or functionality, already implemented. There will be programs for which no choice on the implementation strategy is available.

A program manager must have the same skills as a project manager, skills such as facilitation, communication and leadership. Program managers must also have knowledge and understanding of the organization's strategic goals and objectives, along with an ability to see the big picture across multiple projects. Having the ability to understand and communicate the organization's strategic vision, and the ability to step away from the detailed day-to-day project work, is what helps a project manager move into the program manager role.

A **portfolio** can be described differently among organizations. When referring to projects and programs, a portfolio is a collection of projects and programs. Another definition for the portfolio is the management of the organization's collection of applications and systems. This would include all programs and projects, as well as all work efforts to support and maintain the systems. With either definition, the ultimate goal of the portfolio is to meet strategic objectives.

The portfolio manager must be able to go beyond the management of a single project or program to manage all activities required to implement the systems and to keep them available for the staff to support the mission of the organization.

One goal of the portfolio manager is to maximize the value of the portfolio by evaluating new projects or programs for inclusion. This is an important step when there are competing priorities and limited resources. Ensuring resources are spent on the right IT investments increases fiscal responsibility, especially critical given the limited resource of most healthcare organizations.

As organizations realize the benefits of project management, the next logical step is to build a team of project managers. However, a team of two or more project managers with a focus on managing projects does not necessarily create a **project management office** (PMO).

There are multiple types of PMOs, and they typically provide one or more of the following: project management standards, guidelines, education, mentoring, project auditing, project management-related software and project management resources. The focus is on the centralized and coordinated management of an organization's projects, programs or a combination of both. Therefore, a PMO also may be referred to as a program management office, project office or program office.

The prioritization of new project requests to ensure they are tied to overall business objectives and organizational goals can be completed by the PMO. Often, these decisions are not made by the PMO but rather at a higher level. However, a member of the PMO should be involved in the analysis. While decisions on which projects should be started when based on strategic objectives can be made without input from the PMO, the office needs to be involved to understand the impact of the decision. Their input might include answering questions such as: What will it take to complete the project? Do we have the resources available for this project? Are there competing priorities with current projects underway? Answers to these questions are necessary before a final decision is made to begin something new. Key features and benefits a PMO may provide include:

- Human resources to manage projects.
- Centralized resource for information and communication for all projects.
- A standard methodology followed for all projects.
- A centralized management of project tools, such as project management software, templates and document storage.
- A centralized source for education and mentoring of project managers.
- A coordinated management of overall issues, risks and timelines across all projects within the PMO.
- Assurance that all project work is aligned with the organization's strategic objectives.

Project management is fairly new to the healthcare industry, compared to other industries, such as construction and manufacturing. As more healthcare organizations begin hiring project managers, the concepts of program and portfolio management will become more widespread. PMOs are now emerging within larger healthcare organizations. The keys are to put the right people in the project, program or portfolio manager roles and to have a clear methodology to follow consistently.

CASE STUDY 1
IMPLEMENTATION OF AN ELECTRONIC HEALTH RECORD (EHR)

Type: COTS

Included Functionality

- Allow management and tracking of patient demographics along with admission, discharge and transfer (ADT) information.
- Provide computerized practitioner order entry (CPOE).
- Allow results retrieval (interfaces from lab and radiology information systems).
- Provide clinical documentation for nurses, including an electronic medication administration record (eMAR).

Current Situation

Your organization has just purchased an EHR system from a well-known vendor. You have been assigned to implement this system. Upon review of your current situation, you learn that the current system used for patient demographics and ADT will be replaced with the new EHR. Your laboratory and radiology departments have information systems in which they manually enter the ordered exams and subsequent results. The results are provided to the patient care areas on paper to be placed in the hard copy medical record. All clinical documentation is completed in the paper medical record and is unstructured.

Questions

1. Would this implementation be managed as a project or a program?
2. If managed as a program, how would you break it up into separate related projects?

Feedback

Feedback for this case study can be found in the Appendix.

CASE STUDY 2
IMPLEMENTATION OF AN ORGANIZATIONAL
METRICS DASHBOARD

Type: Custom Development

Included Functionality

- Allow online data entry for defined metrics by staff doing data collection.
- Provide high-level dashboard views of metrics results for executive leadership.
- Provide ability to drill-down into details of any metric in dashboard.

Current Situation

You have been asked to develop software to replace the multiple spreadsheets currently in use to track operational metrics. Upon review of the current situation, you find that the metrics data are currently being collected into separate spreadsheets. The spreadsheets are consolidated and provided to the executive leadership of the organization on a monthly basis. The metrics include a variety of items, such as patient wait times, returns to the operating room, post-procedure infections and quantity of medical and nursing students.

Questions

1. Would this implementation be managed as a project or a program?
2. If managed as a program, how would you break it up into separate related projects?

Feedback

Feedback for this case study can be found in the Appendix.

CHAPTER 3

Project Process Groups

"It takes as much energy to wish as it does to plan."

—Eleanor Roosevelt

Project management is accomplished by applying knowledge and skills while using tools and standard processes to meet project requirements. A project moves through a defined set of **process groups**, with an initial definition of need to the final release of resources. While these process groups are well defined, it is not necessary to apply them consistently across all projects. Because all projects are unique, it is the project manager, along with the project team and sponsors, who determine how each project will move through the process groups.

Every project can be divided into five project management process groups, as depicted below and in Figure 3-1:

1. **Initiating.** This process group defines the business need and authorizes the project.
2. **Planning.** This process group finalizes the project scope and the plan for how to accomplish the objectives to meet the defined need.
3. **Executing.** This process group utilizes project resources to complete the approved project management plan completed in the Planning Process Group.
4. **Monitoring and Controlling.** This process group completes the scheduled quality measures with ongoing monitoring of progress. Identifies variances to the project management plan and associated corrective actions taken to meet the project objectives.
5. **Closing.** This process group formally accepts the product, service or result along with contract and project-closure activities.

Many of these processes are iterative throughout the project's lifecycle. The more the project manager learns about a project, the greater degree of detail there is to be managed. While each process group is defined separately in the project lifecycle, in the real world they often overlap. Planning, for example, is never completely done, since each accepted change, risk or issue requires some level of planning or re-planning.

Most experienced project managers understand that there needs to be some flexibility within the methodology to allow it to be adapted to the individual project. Defined objectives and the complexity that comes from risks, schedule, resources and the amount of historic information further delineates a project's uniqueness. The

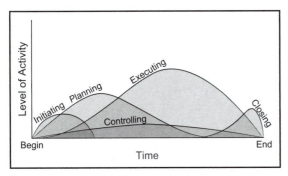

Figure 3-1: The Five Project Management Process Groups.

defined activities and deliverables in each process group should be considered guides, which project managers, with their knowledge and skill, use to determine the best way to apply them to their specific project. There is one constant: each project flows through the entire lifecycle in one form or another.

INITIATING PROCESS GROUP

The **Initiating Process Group** includes all activities that lead up to the formal authorization to begin the new project. These activities are often started, and sometimes even completed, prior to the project manager being assigned. This can lead to the perception that this phase has been skipped, but, in fact, an understanding of the business needs and objectives of the project is always done, even if it is not officially documented. Following a formal process for the analysis and documentation of the different options to meet the business goals ensures that the project that is ultimately authorized will actually meet the need and fit into the organization's strategic objectives.

All projects are approved after some form of analysis or data gathering. Determining the initial definition of need is usually the first step followed by some level of evaluation about what is required to meet the need. A new project request is usually in response to a problem, an opportunity or a new business requirement. Once the initial request is identified and communicated, there should be a consistent process to follow for the evaluation of options and the relationship between the project and the organization's strategic plan. This process is often informal and may not even be documented until the volume of requests causes constraints with budget and resources, at which point a business case may be requested for project justification. Some level of information is necessary for an organization to make the decision to move forward. The best decisions are educated decisions that are made after careful analysis and sound estimates are presented.

Following are possible questions to help evaluate new project requests:
- Why should we do this? What are the benefits to the organization?
- What is the final expected outcome? How does it align with the organizational goals?
- What are the risks if the project is approved? Rejected?
- What is the expected cost, and is this within the budget?

- What assumptions were made when developing the project request?
- What constraints will impact this project?
- What are the expected resources needed to implement this project? Are they available?
- What other options are available for meeting these objectives?

The main deliverable of the Initiating Process Group is the **project charter**. At a very high level, the project charter includes the project objectives, a list of the final deliverables, the estimated duration and a forecast of the resources required.

In multi-phase projects, this process is carried out at the beginning of each phase to validate that the assumptions and decisions from the initial project charter are still accurate. An organization might choose to not require these steps, either because the project has been pre-authorized or is the result of a regulatory requirement that is not optional.

If this is the case, the organization may not require a project charter at all. Instead, it may take the information gathered in this process group and move directly to the planning phase. While this is not a best practice, it does happen. The analysis should still occur even if the formal document is not created, since this information will be used to develop the detailed project management plan.

The objectives of the project, high-level deliverables and high-level resources are defined in the project charter. These lead to further questions about what resources will be needed for the project. Human resources are often defined by what skills or types of staff are necessary for the project team.

The evaluation of current staff will help identify whether these skills are available within the organization or if contract staff are necessary to supplement the project team. Other resources to be considered are new hardware, software, equipment, facilities or supplies. Does this project include the purchase of a software package, or will the project include developing new software? Will there be any license fees that need to be included in the budget?

Understanding what hardware is required for this project, such as workstations or servers, will depend on what is required and what is currently available. All of these answers feed into the estimated budget.

If the project manager is not already involved, he or she should be brought in at this time to work with the stakeholder to create the project charter. While the project management office may help with the development of the charter, the approval and funding are typically external to the team. The project manager and other key stakeholders are involved during this process to ensure shared ownership, buy-in for the process and accurate documentation of the objectives.

The charter is reviewed during the prioritization process that defines which projects will be authorized and when they can begin. Acceptance of the project charter provides formal approval to move forward with the project. At times, the tough decision would be made to not move forward. This might be due to resource constraints, different organizational objectives or competing priorities. However, a project that has gone forward and is now approved moves into the Planning Process Group. If a project manager still has not been identified, it is important to select one now.

Typical contents of the project charter include:
- Project title.
- Estimated start and finish dates.
- Business need, goals and scope.
- Justification and background.
- High-level deliverables.
- Project manager and authorized level of authority.
- Key project stakeholders.
- High-level resources needed.
- Other resources needed.
- High-level milestones and estimated timeline.
- High-level budget estimation.
- SWOT (Strengths, Weaknesses, Opportunities and Threats) analysis.
- Assumptions and constraints.
- Risks and risk management strategy.
- Critical measures of success.

PLANNING PROCESS GROUP

The **Planning Process Group** takes the information gathered and documented during initiation to develop the project management plan. This plan further defines the objectives and then plans the course of action to complete the project. The information in the project charter is only one source used for the detailed planning that occurs during this phase.

Further discussion with the project stakeholders is required to gather and document their specific requirements. In addition, historic documentation from other similar projects can be used as inputs for the planning processes, in which the primary deliverable is the project management plan. The project management plan is actually multiple coordinated documents or plans that define the project and how it will be accomplished. Some documents are consistent across all projects, such as the risk management plan, while others, such as the schedule, are highly unique to each project.

The **project scope** document is less formal and is typically shorter than the project charter. If the project has been approved, an organization might choose to skip the project charter and only require a project scope document. The scope takes the information from the charter and further defines the boundaries of the project to include what will and will not be included, or what is in and out of scope.

Defining what is out of scope can be as important as defining what is in scope. This will help prevent **scope creep** when a decision is made to not include a specific item as part of the project. The project team is identified and their roles within the project are further defined. There are often many unknowns during the planning phase, so any assumptions made should also be documented in the scope. These same assumptions can often feed into any risks that might be identified during this phase.

Members of the **project team** are the SMEs, who not only help the project manager define the contents of the scope but also the remainder of the project management plan. The team provides the details about what activities or tasks are needed to complete the objectives, as well as how long each will take to complete. These details are used to create the **work breakdown structure** (WBS), which some organizations call the work plan. This is the listing of all deliverables and project work, divided into more manageable components and when each will be completed. Resources also are added to each task to define who will be needed and when. This helps the negotiation for project resources to be available when they are needed.

As the plan is defined, it becomes clearer what is required to complete the project. This information feeds into the final project budget that began with the high-level budget produced in the initiation phase. Line items for the budget might include new hardware, software, travel, staff training, facility expenses, license fees, equipment, supplies and supplemental staffing. Some organizations keep track of internal employee salary costs in the budget, while others do not; it is best to work with your finance department to understand their expectations.

One critical piece that is often overlooked is the process to define success factors. There are two parts to this process. The first is to define how to evaluate whether the project is successful. The evaluation of project success is done during the Closing Process Group, even though each deliverable is tested and accepted upon completion. The project success factors, which are focused on the success of the actual project, must be measureable at the end of the project.

The second part is to define how well the project met the business need. This is not easily measured at the end of the project, since the benefits are rarely obtained right away. Often, these are measured over time by analyzing trends that show improvements. These success factors should be defined during the project in the form of a strategic metrics plan that outlines what will be measured, by whom and when. These two concepts will be defined in Chapter 9.

While many plans are unique to each project, some should be used consistently across all projects. The **risk management plan**, **communication management plan**, and **scope management plan** are examples. How risks are identified and managed throughout the project should be consistent; consistency also should be found in the use of any tools used to document the risks and risk responses.

A consistent communication plan ensures that all stakeholders understand how communication will be managed during the project. It is useful to also provide a template that outlines who, what, when and how the project communication will occur that can be filled in for the specific project. This document would reference the communication management plan and provide more details, such as when status meetings will be held and who will be invited to attend.

A change management plan defines how any requests for changes will be managed. While this is often used to control changes to the scope, it should be used for any requested changes, especially for any project document that has been approved. This would relate to documents such as requirements or workflow processes that feed into work assigned further into the project and any change that might have an impact. This plan defines how these requests are managed, the analysis to be completed and who has the authority to approve or deny the requested change. Risks, issues and changes often feed into the iterative reviews of the project management plan.

Each project should have at least one project sponsor. This is the person who provides direction for the project. He or she has the authority to approve the project management plan and any requested changes, assist with aspects that need escalation, and often controls the funding.

Once the project management plan is completed and approved, the project manager schedules a kick-off meeting. The kick-off includes project stakeholders and is held at the end of the Planning Process Group to ensure everyone is aware of what the project is, who will be involved and how it will be completed. This activity ensures the project stakeholders, including the resources assigned during the planning process group, are informed of the contents of the project management plan and how they fit into the success of the project. This is often the final planning activity. (Note: Some organizations hold a kick-off at the beginning of Planning Process Group during which the authorized project is reviewed, and the resources are assigned to begin planning.)

EXECUTING PROCESS GROUP

The **Executing Process Group** occurs when the activities defined in the project management plan are completed. The project manager must coordinate the people and other resources to facilitate completion of the work scheduled. This process group, along with the Monitoring and Controlling Process Group, makes up the longest part (time-wise) of the project, and both process groups occur concurrently.

To keep the schedule on time, the project manager must manage competing priorities and requirements. Scope time, cost and quality must all be balanced to ensure the project is completed on time and on budget. Any change to one of these will impact one, or all, of the others.

The project manager will need to assemble the project team if they have not been brought together already. In some situations, the resources will be fully dedicated to the project, while in others, they may only have a percent of their time allocated to the project. The project manager needs to work within the available parameters to build a cohesive team. It is important to build the group of independent people from various parts of the organization into a team wherein members can trust each other and work together.

The project manager is the primary point of contact for project information. The communication plan outlines the details surrounding the distribution of information. One method of communication with the project team is accomplished through status and ad hoc meetings from which the information is shared through meeting minutes. Working in a virtual environment adds additional challenges in building the team and with team communication.

Sharing information with project stakeholders, who include sponsors and governance committee members, is often accomplished through status reports. These are completed weekly or monthly and provide a high-level account of the project at a single point in time. Communication occurs during these scheduled times, as well as throughout the project.

MONITORING AND CONTROLLING PROCESS GROUP

As mentioned earlier, this process group occurs concurrent to the Executing Process Group. Monitoring the execution of the project management plan helps identify potential problems, and regular measurement of project performance identifies any variances to the plan. Managing changes to the project will help ensure that a change to one area is controlled and integrated across the entire project. When changes are not controlled, the project manager must take corrective action to bring the project back into alignment with the project management plan. With careful monitoring, the project manager can take preventative actions to help avoid variances from occurring.

Periodic evaluation of project performance ensures the quality of the final deliverable. There are many tools that can be used for quality assurance. These include quality audits, along with benchmarking and testing. While it is important to assure the quality of the deliverable, it is also important to validate that the deliverable meets the requirements that were defined and approved. A deliverable that does not meet the requirements is not beneficial, even if it is of high quality. Software testing will be defined in Chapter 7.

Risks identified in the Initiating or Planning Process Groups should be continuously monitored and re-evaluated throughout the project. The defined risk response plans should be updated when new information is obtained. As the timeframe for a risk passes, the risk should be closed. Early identification of new risks ensures timely response planning. Monitoring the conditions that might trigger a risk allows the project manager to quickly implement the response and then evaluate the effectiveness. If risk management is done correctly, it is often unnoticed, since the responses are planned and implemented quickly to resolve problems as they arise.

Tip

If risk management is done correctly, it often goes unnoticed.

Scope creep, a common reason for failed projects, is caused by uncontrolled changes. Any change to the scope or requirements can negatively impact time and cost, as well as every other part of the project. Integrated change control is a formal process to help prevent scope creep. Each change request should be evaluated to understand how it would impact the project, as well as ensuring that it will provide a benefit. Each change should not be undertaken until it is approved.

This approval comes from the project sponsors or governance committee and should be based on the impact analysis, which identifies how the request impacts the scope, budget, schedule and other projects or work within the organization. This process is performed throughout the project, from initiation through closing.

Some projects have defined phases based on the type of work being completed. These phases are unique to the project and should not be confused with process groups. For example, phases in a software implementation might include workflow redesign, system configuration or development, testing, training and activation. At the end of each phase, the deliverables are reviewed to ensure the project is ready to move onto the next phase. These reviews, also called Stage-gate Reviews, ensure the project moves to the next phase only when ready. This is also a good time to perform quality reviews and verify that the project is still on track to meet the scope and requirements defined by the stakeholders.

Earned value management (EVM) is a valuable tool to monitor and control the project schedule and budget. Project managers can evaluate how the project is progressing along the plan related to the schedule and budget. Comparing the estimated schedule and budget to the actual schedule and budget at a single point in time provides a clear picture of the project performance. If a project is behind schedule or over budget, the project manager can utilize the monitoring and controlling tools to help identify the cause and perform corrective action. One of the challenges of utilizing EVM is obtaining real-time data for the budget metrics, since most accounting systems are at least 30 days behind.

CLOSING PROCESS GROUP

The **Closing Process Group** begins once the project deliverables have all been delivered and accepted by the project sponsor(s). For a software project, this refers to the **activation**, or **go-live**, of the software and subsequent use by the end users. Some organizations wait to begin the project closure phase until several weeks after the activation. This allows the project team to focus on supporting end users for a period of time before beginning the closing activities. Once the project work is completed, the project documentation needs to be finalized, and the sponsors formally accept the project deliverables. This formal acceptance of the product, service or result brings the project to an orderly close.

During this process group, all documentation is finalized and archived for use as historical information to future projects. The project team members should be retained in order to finish the project documentation. The final evaluation of project success measures is also completed and documented to demonstrate whether or not the project was successful.

Other activities include the process to finalize and close any remaining contracts. This would include contracts for any products or services related to this project. Bringing project stakeholders together to discuss and evaluate the **lessons learned** from the project provides a valuable retrospective of the project. This increases understanding of what went well that should be repeated in future projects, as well as what could be done better. It is important that the group understands that this is a learning opportunity and not a time to point fingers or apply blame. Rather, this exercise provides the ability to continuously learn from one project to another to improve processes.

Formal acceptance of the project is typically completed through a formal document that evaluates the original project scope and approved changes against what actually was delivered at the end of the project. Do they accept the final product as is and did it include all requirements defined at the beginning of the project? Once this acceptance is obtained and all documentation is completed and archived, it is time to celebrate successful completion of the project. The celebration is the final activity before the resources are released and the project is considered complete.

All projects move through these five process groups during their lifecycles. The amount of time spent in each process group and the exact activities included are dependent on the uniqueness of the project itself. The project manager should utilize a standard methodology that allows for tailoring based on the project need. A software project also will include at least a portion of the software lifecycle, which flows from identification of requirements through to when it is turned off and no longer in use. This lifecycle is defined in Chapter 5.

CASE STUDY 1
IMPLEMENTATION OF AN ELECTRONIC HEALTH RECORD (EHR)

Type: COTS

Additional Information

The vendor offers a full suite of functionality and modules for the hospital, which includes a standard interface for lab and radiology, but your organization has not developed these interfaces before. The nurses use a paper medication administration form, but clinical documentation is free text without any standard structure. Physicians use order forms for writing patient medical orders that are processed by unit staff, with copies sent to the necessary departments.

Questions

1. What types of training might be included in the training plan for this project/program?
2. What might be some challenges faced by the project/program team?
3. What roles, or skill sets, would be required for the project/program team?

Feedback

Feedback for this case study can be found in the Appendix.

CASE STUDY 2
IMPLEMENTATION OF AN ORGANIZATIONAL METRICS DASHBOARD

Type: Custom Development

Additional Information

There are a limited number of people, approximately 15, who collect the metrics data on a set schedule. The frequency of the different measurements varies from weekly to annually. One goal identified early is for the new system to be Web-based for easy access.

Questions

1. What types of training might be included in the training plan for this project/program?
2. What might be some challenges faced by the project/program team?
3. What roles or skill sets would be required for the project/program team?

Feedback

Feedback for this case study can be found in the Appendix.

CHAPTER 4

Project Knowledge Areas

"True motivation comes from achievement, personal development, job satisfaction, and recognition."

—Frederick Herzberg

The Project Management Institute (PMI) identifies nine knowledge areas that contain processes to be accomplished for effective project management. Some lead to specific project objectives, such as scope, cost, time and quality management. Others provide methods to achieve the objectives, such as those related to human resource, communication, procurement and risk management.

The one knowledge area that is influenced by and influences all others is **integration management**. Project managers must have knowledge and skills in each of these areas or have specialists who can assist in these areas. For example, some large projects have dedicated schedule coordinators, risk managers, communication specialists or procurement contract officers.

Each of the five project management process groups defined in Chapter 3 can be mapped to these management knowledge areas. Table 4-1 demonstrates this mapping.

Project Integration Management
Initiating Process Group
• Develop project charter.
Planning Process Group
• Develop project management plan.
Executing Process Group
• Execution of the project management plan.
Monitoring & Controlling Process Group
• Monitor and control project activities.
• Perform change control.
Closing Process Group
• Close project.

Table 4-1: Relationship Between Knowledge Areas and Process Groups.

Project Scope Management

Planning Process Group
- Collect and document requirements.
- Define project scope.
- Create WBS.

Monitoring & Controlling Process Group
- Verify scope.
- Scope change control.

Project Time Management

Planning Process Group
- Define activities.
- Sequence activities.
- Estimate activity resources.
- Estimate activity durations.
- Develop schedule.

Monitoring & Controlling Process Group
- Control schedule.

Project Cost Management

Planning Process Group
- Resource planning.
- Estimate costs.
- Define budget.

Monitoring & Controlling Process Group
- Control costs.

Project Quality Management

Planning Process Group
- Quality planning.

Executing Process Group
- Quality assurance.

Monitoring & Controlling Process Group
- Quality control.

Project Human Resource Management

Planning Process Group
- Develop human resource plan.
- Organizational planning.
- Staff acquisition.

Table 4-1: *(Continued)*

Project Human Resource Management

Executing Process Group
- Develop project team.
- Manage project team.

Closing Process Group
- Release resources.

Project Communications Management

Initiating Process Group
- Identify stakeholders.

Planning Process Group
- Develop communication plan.

Executing Process Group
- Distribute information.
- Manage stakeholder expectations.

Monitoring & Controlling Process Group
- Report performance.

Closing Process Group
- Administrative closure.

Project Risk Management

Planning Process Group
- Define risks management plan.
- Identify risks.
- Perform qualitative and quantitative risk analysis.
- Develop responses.

Monitoring & Controlling Process Group
- Monitor and control risks.

Project Procurement Management

Planning Process Group
- Plan procurements.
- Plan solicitation.

Executing Process Group
- Solicitation.
- Source selection.
- Contract administration.

Monitoring & Controlling Process Group
- Monitor and control contracts.

Closing Process Group
- Contract close-out.

Table 4-1: *(Continued)*

INTEGRATION MANAGEMENT

Integration management is used in project management to coordinate activities that occur across all of the process groups and knowledge areas. The ability to look beyond any single activity or decision to see how it will impact the rest of the project is necessary to keep the work on track. Monitoring and controlling project performance and the ability to be flexible when a decision or risk may impact multiple aspects of the project are important parts of integration management.

The main activities that occur during integration management involve the development and management of the **project management plan**. This is a clear, concise plan for how the project will be completed. The management and control of activities included in the plan, ensuring they are executed as scheduled, is also part of this knowledge group. Controlling all project changes involves coordinating changes across the entire project. This would include changes introduced by stakeholder requests, risks, issues or changes in the organization's strategic objectives that might impact the project.

Tip

Changes will happen and should be expected.

Someone must focus on the big picture and take responsibility for the overall coordination of the project, and this becomes a top function of project managers who must also be able to keep their focus on multiple fronts at the same time. They need to have one eye on the day-to-day activities to ensure their timely completion, while keeping the other eye on the bigger picture to manage and control the overall project. This leads some people to feel that integration management is the key to overall project success.

SCOPE MANAGEMENT

Proper scope definition and management does not guarantee a successful project, but studies show that not determining these appropriately in the early stages is a main reason for project failure. Defining scope is a difficult activity, especially when many people are providing input. Project stakeholders must come to consensus about what will and will not be included in the scope. Once defined and approved, it is the project manager's role to ensure that the entire team has the same understanding of the scope and how the final outcomes will be delivered.

The main processes in the **scope management** knowledge area start with the project scope statement within the project charter, and are elaborated with the definition and documentation of project functional requirements. The project's functional requirements define the *what* that is needed in the project. However, these requirements are often gathered from stakeholders who frequently provide the *how* rather than the *what*. It takes a unique skill to obtain the true requirements from the project stakeholders who, in many cases, often are not sure what they want.

When purchasing a COTS system from a vendor, the requirements are often gathered and documented as part of the **procurement process**. With this example, the requirements are frequently related to what functionality will be implemented, how the functionality will be customized or specifics required for developing an interface between two or more systems.

If the project involves developing custom software, the requirements are obtained during planning. These requirements are usually a two-step process. The **business requirements** are provided by the stakeholders and define what they want the new system to do. These are followed by system requirements, which define the details about how the system will be developed to meet the business requirements. Clear and well-defined requirements are as important as a clear and well-defined scope; without either, the end product will not meet the business need or the stakeholders' expectations. Once requirements are collected and documented and a detailed description of the project is obtained, the WBS is developed.

Scope change control involves controlling changes to the project scope. Each change request should be analyzed to determine the impact it will have on the project, as well as on any other projects in the organization's portfolio. Once the impact analysis is complete, an educated decision is made to accept or reject the change. The key is not to prevent changes, but rather control them and ensure the impact is known before they are accepted. Change management does not only refer to the scope. Changes to requirements, once approved, can have the same impact on the project, even if the changes don't impact the scope. It is important for the project manager to control all changes within the project.

TIME MANAGEMENT

Completing a project on time is a common measure of success, and also one of the biggest challenges. Issues with the schedule tend to cause the most conflicts across the project lifecycle. Once a project schedule is set and communicated, it is often the most common measurement of project performance. Comparing planned activity times with actual activity times to determine if a project is on time should take into account modifications to the schedule from approved changes. Time also is the one true constant and continues no matter what happens on the project.

Project **time management** involves all activities related to completing the project. While this sounds simple, it is far from easy and it all begins with proper planning. The project manager works with the SMEs within the project team to identify the tasks necessary to complete the scope and project deliverables.

Identification of the activities includes the expected work effort, duration, cost, resource requirements and activity sequencing. Obtaining the actual activities, or tasks, from the SMEs can sometimes be as much of an art form as obtaining requirements from stakeholders. As these are defined, the relationships between activities must be understood to ensure proper sequencing.

Tip

> Be careful when communicating project activation or end dates, because they may change during long projects. Instead, provide stakeholders an approximate date range. As the project progresses, you can refine and specify dates.

With most healthcare organizations, the project resources may not be dedicated to one specific project, so the difference between work effort and duration can be challenging to define. Often the resources are supporting other systems while helping to implement the new one and may even be working on multiple projects. This provides challenges to controlling the schedule when an issue with a current system can be a higher priority than project work.

When implementing a COTS system, the vendor can assist with the activity definition, based on their past experiences with other clients. They often know what activities are necessary and what detailed tasks are needed to complete them. Defining these activities when developing new software is not as straightforward. The development model utilized will impact the activities involved. Will a prototype be developed? Will they develop and deliver the software in phases? Software development is a more cyclical process, during which a portion of the development is completed and shown to the customer who provides feedback. This feedback is reviewed and more development is completed, and again is shown to the customer. This process tends to add some complexity to developing and controlling the schedule. How many times will this cycle occur? If requirements were not documented well or the customer is not sure what they want, this can go on for many cycles, making it difficult to identify the end of the project. This is often the difference between selecting a system where you can see the functionality and how it works vs. trying to define every detail of what you want without being able to see functionality and its process up front.

Once the schedule is completed and approved, it must be controlled as with any other portion of the project. Any change to the project can affect the schedule, although it is important to note that not all changes will increase the timeline; some will decrease the schedule as an outcome of the change and some changes that are made because of the need to complete the project sooner.

COST MANAGEMENT

Information technology projects can be expensive, and even escalate way over budget. If you are unable to obtain good requirements or good estimations of activities, the project budget will be difficult to get right. Most IT projects include new technology or new business processes. If these are untested, their use can lead to risks that cause increased costs, whereas well-defined projects, using proven technology and accurate time estimates, can lead to realistic budgets. Depending on the amount of risk and confidence in the schedule, the budget could include an amount of money set aside as part of the contingency plan.

When purchasing a COTS system from a vendor, the budget usually includes only the costs from that vendor. This will often include software licenses, services to assist with implementation and possibly hardware, depending on the vendor and contract. What the budget often does not include is internal costs, such as the organization's resources that will be assigned to the project. Will this project utilize currently owned hardware or software? What human resources will be used? It is an organization's decision whether to include these costs in the project budget. When they are not included, it is because these resources are already part of the organization's larger budget, therefore, no increased cost is incurred from their use on this project.

The costs for software development tend to be more variable. The reliability of the requirements will feed into the reliability of the budget. There is a higher risk in software development of not meeting the customer's needs, which then requires rework and longer timelines. There can also be a learning curve if new technology is utilized for development. On top of these considerations, there remain some of the same issues as already discussed, even if the development work is done within the organization or through a contract with another company. A good project manager needs to understand basic cost management concepts to help control the budget. This relates to organizations in which the project budget is managed by the project manager or managed elsewhere, such as through the finance department.

QUALITY MANAGEMENT

As quality can be defined so many different ways, it is important to understand how the stakeholders define quality related to this particular project. Some see quality as the final outcome being in compliance with the project's requirements. Others focus on how well the final product meets the intended use. Conforming to requirements and fitness for use are only two ways to define quality. The primary purpose of **quality management** is to ensure that the final product meets the business need. Some measures of quality are measurable during the project, while others cannot be measured for months after the project ends. It is important to remember that the customer decides if the quality of final product is acceptable.

The quality planning process includes identifying the quality standards that are related to this specific project and how they will be met. For IT projects, this might relate to response time, accuracy of the data, or the amount of time the system is available, or uptime. The quality assurance process evaluates the project performance based on the quality standards defined in the quality management plan. There are many tools and techniques available to help with quality control in which specific results are measured through inspections of deliverables based on metrics defined and approved in the quality management plan. Quality planning defines how quality will be measured; quality control is the actual testing; and quality assurance is the evaluation of the quality process in relation to the project.

One important technique to measure quality for IT projects is often considered a phase in the project's lifecycle. Most testing occurs after the development of a software component or at the completion of all development. The different types of testing are defined in Chapter 7. Testing can validate all requirements are met, that the performance meets expectations and/or how well the system fits with the redesigned workflow. Testing resources include the actual developers, testers and even the end users. All have a role in proper testing prior to activation or go-live.

HUMAN RESOURCE MANAGEMENT

Human resource management in projects is a vital skill for all project managers. A team will often consist of people brought together for the first time, and it is the project manager's job to form them into a team that will work together to complete the project. High-level resource needs are identified in the project charter and the needs are further refined during the planning phase. The process of acquiring the necessary skills for the project team varies depending on the organization. Negotiating for the staff's time to work on the project, when they are needed, can be challenging, especially when there are competing priorities. During this process, the project roles and responsibilities are defined.

Once the team is assigned, team development should occur as soon as possible. Even the most talented individuals must learn to work as a team to achieve the project's goals. To be effective, they need to be able to utilize their individual strengths while working with others. There are a variety of team-building activities available. If there is a cost for these activities, they should be considered early enough to be included in the budget to ensure adequate funding. Training for the project team on the new software or technology should also be identified during the planning phase, and is often required prior to or at the beginning of the execution phase.

The project manager will need to work closely with the team member's human resource manager, unless the organization has a project organizational structure, wherein the team reports directly to the project manager. This collaboration helps prioritize conflicts among team members. The project manager should have the opportunity to provide input into the team members' performance reviews. In this situation, the project manager has the authority to direct the staff's work, but only within the project.

COMMUNICATIONS MANAGEMENT

Communication is more than distributing information. It involves understanding the information received and being able to explain it to others. It is well known that IT professionals have their own terminology that is not often understood by outsiders. This is also true with the healthcare industry. There needs to be someone on the team who can understand both sides and help translate when needed. **Informatics**, a healthcare discipline that is growing rapidly, blends information science, computer science and healthcare. The ability to help with communication is only one benefit informatics can bring to the project team.

When the stakeholders are identified, the project manager should understand how each would contribute to the project. This analysis feeds into the communication plan, ensuring that the right information is shared with the right people at the right time using the right communication vehicle. Even though the project manager is often the hub of the project's communication, distributing information, such as the status of tasks, newly identified risks or issues and the resolution of current issues, is part of every team member's responsibility. The reporting of project performance includes regular status reports to stakeholders, governance committees and project team members. These are often snapshots in time, communicating how the project is progressing with what activities have been completed and what is scheduled for the next time period. They also include new risks and issues that need to be escalated. This communication helps manage stakeholder expectations and should include the information they ask for based on their interest in the project.

During the closing phase, the project manager must ensure that all project documentation is completed and archived. Team members should not be released until all project documentation is completed to ensure they are available to provide details necessary for this step. The administrative closure documentation is completed by the project manager and involves formal acceptance of the project by the stakeholders. This documentation becomes historical information for future projects.

RISK MANAGEMENT

Risk management is the process of identifying, analyzing and responding to risks throughout the project. Early identification of risks is the responsibility of all project team members and is critical, as the earlier risks are identified the more time there is to perform risk analysis and plan the risk response. Communication of risks to stakeholders helps them understand the nature of the project and helps with managing their expectations. Proper risk management is a form of insurance to lessen the impact of potential adverse events. This is the area in which most organizations can improve project performance.

Most organizations struggle for a balance between risk and opportunity. The opportunity that comes from a new system must be weighed against the risks. Different organizations have different risk tolerances. Do you want to be on the leading edge of technology, willing to take additional risk to be the first to implement and use new technology? Your organization would be a risk-seeker.

At the other end of the spectrum are the risk-adverse, who have a lower tolerance for risk and want to play it safe. A risk-adverse organization prefers to implement technology after it has been proven to be stable and reliable. The middle ground is risk-neutral, the point at which the organization seeks a balance between risk and benefit.

Risk analysis looks to evaluate each risk to estimate the probability of occurrence and the impact to the project. Quantifying risks help the project manager prioritize them to determine the threshold for which risks deserve the most attention. Ones with a higher probability of occurrence with a higher impact to the project should be carefully monitored.

After the analysis, the organization must decide on a response for each risk. Eliminating the risk, often by removing the cause, is an example of risk avoidance. **Risk avoidance** requires a change to the project to remove the cause of the risk, such as eliminating a deliverable, modifying the requirement or changing a member of the project team. **Risk acceptance** occurs when the organization accepts the consequences if the risk occurs because they either cannot do anything to avoid it or the impact is minimal. When a risk is accepted, a contingency plan should be developed and funds set aside to support the contingency plan.

Reducing the impact or probability of the risk event is a method of risk mitigation; if the impact is high enough, the project manager may attempt to do both. Any risk mitigation activities should be added to the project schedule.

Risk management continues throughout the project by monitoring and controlling identified risks and associated mitigation activities. As the project progresses, new risks can be identified and analyzed. Some risks can be closed before the project ends. For example, the risk that the hardware will not arrive on time can be closed after the hardware is delivered and verified to be what was ordered.

PROCUREMENT MANAGEMENT

Procurement is a term used by the government to describe obtaining goods or services from an outside source. Others use the terms purchasing, contracting or outsourcing. In some organizations, procurement management may also be called contract management. It is important to understand that the procurement process includes more than just managing contracts. It also includes planning, proposal development, proposal response evaluation, negotiation through management of the awarded contract and proper contract closure.

Organizations purchase software from vendors, such as a surgery system, a pharmacy system or a full EHR system. Outsourcing also is used to acquire temporary staffing to supplement the in-house staff on a project when the necessary skill set is not available; for example, most healthcare organizations do not have developers on staff to build custom software. Whether purchasing a system from a vendor or contracting to develop one, new hardware is often also needed. These purchases need to be managed as part of the project.

Procurement planning involves determining what to purchase. The first step includes defining what the requirements are for the purchase. If it is unclear what is available, a market analysis can be conducted. This analysis can lead a make-or-buy decision. If there isn't a vendor that can meet the organization's requirements, it might be decided to build rather than buy.

Solicitation planning includes the development of a **request for proposal** (RFP). This document includes full requirements to ensure the selected vendor can meet them. If the requirements are not clear or complete, the new system may end up not being acceptable. Source selection occurs after each RFP response is evaluated and the contract is negotiated. Each organization has its own processes for who is involved in these activities, as well as what occurs at each step. The process also differs between the public and private sectors. The need to be objective and unbiased is required for anyone participating in procurement management.

Sometimes the vendor's staff is brought in to work beside the organization's staff on the project team. Managing the relationship with the vendor is part of contract administration and part of managing the project team. Who manages the contract is dependent upon the organization; it can be the project manager or a member of the contracting office. Even if the contracting office does the management, the project manager is the person who confirms that the activities are completed and milestones are met on schedule that leads to contract payments. During the closing phase, all contracted deliverables are confirmed and all open items are resolved. Once formal acceptance is completed, the contract is closed out.

Each of these knowledge areas span the five process groups. They describe the activities that the project manager facilitates throughout the project. Table 4-1 shows how the process groups and knowledge areas are interrelated.

CASE STUDY 1
IMPLEMENTATION OF AN ELECTRONIC HEALTH RECORD (EHR)

Type: COTS

Additional Information

The vendor provides a standard WBS work plan that outlines a 16-month implementation plan. The new hardware has been ordered. They have assigned the following resources:

- **Project Manager:** To manage vendor work and resources.
- **Trainer:** To provide training for project team and super users.
- **Clinical Consultant:** To facilitate workflow redesign.
- **Configuration Consultant:** To provide guidance and assistance for system build and customization.
- **Technical Specialist:** To provide guidance and assistance for the technical configuration related to hardware and database.
- **Technical Interface Specialist:** To provide guidance and assistance for the interface development.

Questions

1. What types of requirements are needed for this project/program?
2. What types of line items would you expect to find on the budget?
3. Who would you expect to be stakeholders for this project/program?
4. What methods of communication might the project manager utilize for this project/program?

Feedback

Feedback for this case study can be found in the Appendix.

CASE STUDY 2
IMPLEMENTATION OF AN ORGANIZATIONAL METRICS DASHBOARD

Type: Custom Development

Additional Information

The project sponsor has identified three key people with whom the team should work to define requirements. They will be the super users who can also assist with testing. An experienced developer from the IT department will develop the new system. He will develop a platform in use for other systems and host it on current servers in the data center.

Questions

1. What types of requirements are needed for this project/program?
2. What types of line items would you expect to find on the budget?
3. Who would you expect to be stakeholders for this project/program?
4. What methods of communication might the project manager utilize for this project/program?

Feedback

Feedback for this case study can be found in the Appendix.

CHAPTER 5

Software Development Lifecycle

"Any fool can write code that a computer can understand. Good programmers write code that humans can understand."

—Martin Fowler

The process of developing software has become more complex over the years. This has led to the development of multiple models of the **software development lifecycle** (SDLC). The SDLC defines the phases a system goes through, from initially being conceived until it is discarded.

The initial model was called **Waterfall**, followed by others, such as **Spiral**, **Rapid Prototype** and **Incremental**. Each phase of the software development lifecycle has an output that becomes the input to the next. The Waterfall Model is well understood but a little outdated, as it assumes all requirements are known up front and that each stage is completed prior to moving on to the next stage. The newer models identify the need for a more iterative approach.

The Spiral Model is actually a series of Waterfall cycles. This approach demonstrates proof-of-concept early in the development cycle. With each model, the phases may be given a variety of names, but they are fairly consistent: requirements, analysis or specification, design, construction or development, validation or testing, installation, operations and maintenance and retirement. There is no single SDLC model that is correct.

There are many important aspects of developing software. Clear, concise and accurate requirements are probably the most challenging. Early stakeholder involvement when defining the project scope and system requirements helps to build ownership in the process and the final product. But stakeholder involvement is not enough to ensure that the requirements are accurately documented. A strong business or systems analyst has the skills to obtain the requirements when, as is often the case, the stakeholders are not sure what they want, at least not to the level of detail necessary for the developers.

Often, requirements are documented in two phases. They start with the business requirements for which the functionality being requested is defined, the *what*. These are followed by the technical requirements, or system design, which outlines the details around how the system will be developed to meet the business requirements, or the *how*. These are sometimes referred to as the "specs." This process includes screen layouts, business rules, process diagrams and mock-ups of any reports or outputs. It is often hard to develop software that completely matches the stakeholders' perception of what they asked for. Unlike a COTS system, they cannot look at something and say, "We like this feature, but not that one." This is one of the leading reasons the development models have moved to an iterative development approach. Each version can be verified prior to moving further. The ultimate goal is to develop a system that meets or exceeds the customer's expectations.

Walkthroughs are used to review documentation, such as the specifications or design. The documents are sent out to the walkthrough team prior to the meeting, so they can be reviewed individually. During the walkthrough meeting, the areas that require clarification or that are identified as incorrect are discussed. The process can be done by each person reviewing his or her notes or by going through the document from start to finish, with the team providing input throughout. The latter tends to be more comprehensive. The focus of walkthroughs is to identify incorrect items, so they can be brought back to the appropriate team member to resolve.

A process that is similar to walkthroughs but is more formal is an **inspection**. This is completed by inspecting the design or actual development code, looking for errors. An overview of the item being inspected is provided prior to distributing for review. During the inspection meeting, each item is covered at least once to ensure full review. As with walkthroughs, the focus is on identifying errors, not correcting them. A written report is produced listing all errors found, which is provided to the appropriate staff for rework. When all items are resolved, there is follow-up to ensure all corrections are checked.

Once all requirements and designs are approved, the development begins. This includes actually programming the code that is the base for the system. The developer often completes unit testing during this phase. If one of the iterative models is used, prototypes will be shown to the stakeholders at key points in the development process. This validation step helps to ensure that what is expected is what is being developed. Any requested changes to the requirements are completed through a formal change management process and are completed only after approval.

 Tip

The *product* lifecycle lasts the entire life of the product, from initial concept through retirement, but the *project* lifecycle only lasts as long as the project.

The system is tested at various stages through the lifecycle, depending on the SDLC model and the project management plan. As mentioned earlier, unit testing occurs during development and further testing follows. If a prototype is accepted, functional testing may follow while other development proceeds or may wait for all development to be completed. The test plan is defined during the planning phase of the project and outlines exactly what types of testing will be included and when each will occur. The testing includes validation of the final product against the requirements, as well as verifying the quality of the system against any bugs or issues. The different types of testing, which are part of the quality control process, are defined in Chapter 7.

Testing is followed by stakeholder acceptance and deployment or activation. The stakeholders should accept the system prior to it being deployed into a production environment and the end users begin using it. This is often accomplished through a series of go/no-go meetings during which the system's operational readiness is reviewed. These reviews include the status of any last-minute activities, outstanding issues, or bugs, as well as any go/no-go criteria defined earlier in the project. During this time, planning is occurring for the activation, or go-live. This activity is often forgotten until the very end and there is little time left for planning. Management of the activation activities is defined in Chapter 8.

Once the system is live, it needs to be transitioned to operations and maintenance. Who will support the software once in use? What is the process for end users to request modifications or report issues? System changes should follow a standard change management process to ensure that only approved changes are made and the proper documentation and testing occur for each change prior to migrating it to the production system.

 Tip

> While there are many models for developing software, there is not a single one that is right for all situations.

WATERFALL MODEL

The Waterfall Model, as depicted in Figure 5-1 is the original software development lifecycle model. Each phase is clearly defined and must be completed prior to moving on to the next. This starts with gathering the requirements, which are verified by the stakeholders or a group identified by the stakeholders. The specification phase is the documentation of the functionality required within the system. Once the specification document is approved, the project management plan for development is defined. Once the stakeholders approve the project management plan, the design phase begins.

During the design phase, if something is unclear or incomplete, the work stops and the project moves back to the specification phase in a feedback loop until the specifications and design are verified. The implementation phase also includes a feedback loop that allows for modifications to be made to the requirements, specification document, or even the design document, as necessary. Modules are developed, implemented, tested and then integrated with each other to form the complete system.

The vast majority of a system budget is spent on operations and maintenance, from implementation through retirement. Proper planning for this phase is necessary, and the disciplined approach continues well after the initial development is over. This model does include full documentation and stakeholder approval before moving on to the next phase.

The advantages of the Waterfall Model include a disciplined approach that is enforced through the required documentation and verification for each phase. The milestone ending each phase is the verification of all deliverables, including documentation, by the stakeholders or their designees. Testing is inherent to each phase, so this activity occurs throughout the process and not in its own phase after development. This emphasis on documentation can be a disadvantage if the stakeholders are verifying and approving documents that they do not understand or don't take the time to read thoroughly. An example of a Waterfall Model is depicted in Figure 5-1.

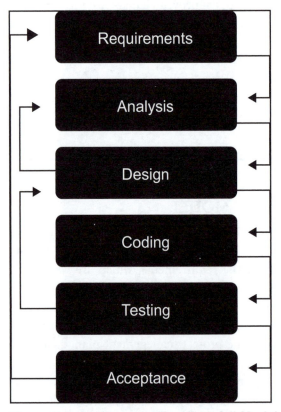

Figure 5-1: An Example of a Waterfall Model.

SPIRAL MODEL

The Spiral Model, as depicted in Figure 5-2, is a modified version of the waterfall designed to decrease the risks surrounding software development by the use of prototypes and risk analysis. Each phase begins with an analysis of the risks at that time. Each significant risk should be resolved before proceeding to the next phase. The use of prototypes alone helps reduce risks. With each prototype representing specific functionality, the verification of project durations and requirements are more easily measured. Each cycle of the spiral depicts a phase of this iterative development lifecycle, with prototypes developed at different phases. The focus on multiple prototypes minimizes scope creep and focuses the work effort on management project pieces.

There are many advantages to the Spiral Model. The emphasis on risk analysis and prototypes provide validation that the project is on schedule and meeting requirements. Maintenance is another cycle in the spiral, so this is treated the same as the initial development. This model lends itself to large-scale development projects. This is because the cost of multiple risk analyses can overshadow some smaller projects that may have much smaller budgets.

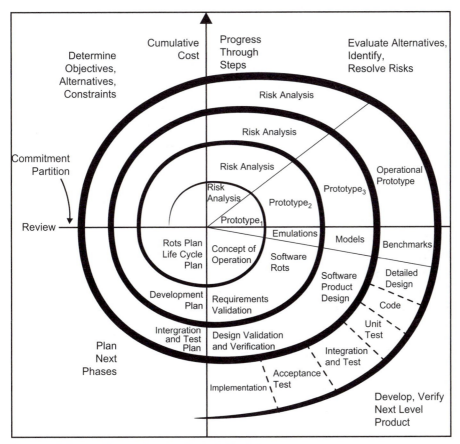

Figure 5-2: An Example of a Spiral Model.

RAPID PROTOTYPE MODEL

This model begins with a rapid prototype, or working model of a portion of the final system. The rapid prototype should be developed quickly to speed up the development process. This is provided to the stakeholders or end users to experiment with and utilize to verify that it meets their needs. Once the real requirements are verified, the prototype is often discarded. This phase is followed with phases similar to the Waterfall Model with specification, design, implementation and integration prior to operations and retirement. This model provides rapid validation of requirements, but can extend the length of development over the traditional Waterfall Model.

INCREMENTAL MODEL

The Incremental Model builds software during each of the steps. Each step, or increment, goes through the same processes until the final system is complete. The initial phases are similar to the other models, starting with requirements, specification and design. Each incremental build goes through detailed design, implementation, integration, testing and delivery to the end users. These phases are repeated over and over again until all pieces are delivered and all requirements are met.

During planning, the number and content of the incremental builds are determined. They should be significant enough to provide sufficient new functionality to avoid spending an exceptional amount of time with regression testing for the benefits provided. This model provides a functioning at the end of each incremental build, but with only a portion of the functionality requested. This allows the end users to begin using the system earlier than with the other models, but only a portion of what they need at a time and each incremental build needs to be integrated with the previous versions. This does allow the ability to terminate the development at any time with some benefit delivered.

When purchasing a COTS system, the vendor has already gone through the initial phases of the development lifecycle. The requirements were gathered from SMEs who are employed by the vendor, are contractors or work for organizations partnering with the vendor. The system is in the operations phase and is available for purchase. These types of systems are not custom developed for one specific need, rather they have been developed to meet a general need within the marketplace. These are systems that can be used within the emergency department, radiology department, a physician's practice or throughout the organization, such as an EHR. They can also be smaller niche systems, such as for nurse scheduling or physician credentialing. These systems are typically delivered with basic functionality and with the capability for the customer to customize them for their unique needs and workflows.

Implementing a COTS system follows a similar lifecycle. Understanding the business need is always the first step. Since the implementation begins with the purchase of the system, the beginning is usually focused on the procurement process. This process can vary between organizations, public and private sectors, and when there is a previous agreement with the vendor, such as adding a new module to a current system. The activity of gathering and understanding the requirements is necessary early in the process for market research to find out whether any systems are available to meet the need. This helps with the decision to buy or build.

Once the new system has been purchased, the project planning begins. The vendor should provide resources to assist with the implementation of the system and guidance on what activities are standard, based on past experience with other clients. During this phase, the organization should make a decision about what functionality will be implemented and when. The project scope should identify whether all available functionality will be implemented as part of the project or not. If not all features will be used; these should be clearly noted in the project scope. The implementation plan should also include the activation strategy. Will this system go live all at once, as a Big Bang? Will it go live in phases, one module or section of the organization at a time?

During planning, it is important to remember that workflows will change and enough time needs to be scheduled for process redesign activities. When documenting the current workflows, remember that documented processes or procedures do not always match what really happens. The real workflows need to be documented to understand how they might change when the new system is implemented.

When moving to any form of automation, the workflows will change. Benefits and efficiencies are not realized when workflows are automated as they are, they should be improved. Representatives of end users must be involved in the process redesign activities to ensure the future workflows will fit into their daily work. The documented future workflows feed into testing scenarios, as well as training materials and provide guidance for post-live support.

The vendor can assist with defining the activities surrounding the configuration of the system. This phase is similar to the build or development phase of the SDLC. Most systems on the market allow for some configuration based on the unique organizational processes. The more customization allowed, the better the system will fit within the organization's processes, but the longer this phase will last. These can be simple items, such as defining the format for the date and time, or they can be more complex, such as configuring structured notes for clinical documentation.

The contract with the vendor should define who would be assigned to do these activities. Will the vendor do all configurations based on decisions made by the organization or will they provide training and guidance to allow the organization's IT or clinical staff to complete these activities? Either way, the project manager and procurement officer should manage the contract to ensure everything is delivered and completed as defined.

All systems go through a software development lifecycle, from initial identification of need through termination. The organization is actively involved in this process for custom developed software that is built for their specific needs. When the organization purchases a new system to fill the need, the system has already gone through most of the development lifecycle. There is still a need to go through similar phases to identify and complete the customization prior to testing and activation.

CASE STUDY 1
IMPLEMENTATION OF AN ELECTRONIC HEALTH RECORD (EHR)

Type: COTS

Additional Information

The vendor has provided details about how the new system can be customized. The organization can decide and build the following:

- Forms used for physician orders.
- How orders are displayed once entered.
- Format used for clinical documentation.
- How clinical documentation is displayed once entered.
- How results will be displayed when posted from the interfaces.
- How medication orders will be posted for documentation on the eMAR.
- Reports to be displayed and printed from the system.

Question

1. What phases would this project/program include?

Feedback

Feedback for this case study can be found in the Appendix.

CASE STUDY 2
IMPLEMENTATION OF AN ORGANIZATIONAL METRICS DASHBOARD

Type: Custom Development

Additional Information

The following functionality is being requested:

1. Allow direct data entry for 10 specific metrics collected throughout the organization.
2. Provide the ability to load the past two years' worth of data.
3. Provide dashboard views of data with the ability to click on any value to view more detailed data.

Question

1. What phases would this project/program include?

Feedback

Feedback for this case study can be found in the Appendix.

CHAPTER 6

System Configuration

"Hope is not a strategy. We have to plan."
—Julie Gerberding, MD, former director of the Centers for Disease
Control and Prevention

Some say project managers do not necessarily need to have knowledge of the industry or subject of the project to manage it. Others respond that while it is not necessary, it is beneficial to have a basic understanding of the industry or subject to have credibility with project team members and to know what to ask and how to gauge the answers.

To fulfill this latter skill set, this chapter will provide an overview of the more common technical concepts and terms used when implementing software. In addition to the information provided here, it is highly beneficial to find one or two people who can serve as references, providing explanations of unknown concepts and terms as the project progresses. This source of information would not necessarily be members of the project team.

Tip

Project managers should be able to trust their project team members to be the SMEs. Unfortunately, project managers rarely get to choose their team members.

Workstations

When implementing a new system, the project team should evaluate the availability of workstations for the end users. The evaluation should include the locations at which the systems will be used. If there are **workstations** present in this location, are they correctly situated and configured to fit with the workflow? If additional workstations are needed, is there space, is there power and is network access available? Further, do the current workstations meet the specifications of the system? For example, a picture archiving and communication system (PACS) used to view electronic radiology images may require extra memory and a high-resolution monitor to meet specs.

Client

A **client** is an application that enables a user (human, service, interface) to access the central information store or database. This access can be requested by a human using the system connected to the database, a service requesting data from the database or an interface requesting or sending data to the database. This is essentially the client-server model, which will be further defined later in this chapter. The client makes requests whether to send or receive data and the server satisfies that request.

A **thin client** is a computer or application that relies on other hardware for most of the traditional computational work. The end user accesses the system through a low-end computer terminal—or dumb terminal—while the server provides the processing and storage functionality.

Multiple terminals can access the same server to run the system. The benefits of this technology are the lower cost and easier maintenance of the terminal workstations. Updates to the system only need to be made on the server rather than to the individual workstations. While the server is very robust and can handle multiple clients, the performance tends to be variable, depending on the application configuration and infrastructure. The server can also become a single point of failure.

The thinnest clients are remote desktop applications at which the systems are running on a centrally hosted virtual workstation. An example of a thin client is an Internet browser connected to the Web site, like Amazon.com. A thin client can be platform independent, which means the user is not restricted to only using a specific type of computer or operating system.

There are a variety of vendors who can provide thin client technology for the healthcare industry. The user needs no special software to access the system and to receive or send data.

The contrast is the traditional **thick** or **fat client** in which most processing and storage functions for the system are done by the workstation, rather than by relying on other hardware. These systems usually require higher processing power and high-resolution graphics cards. This option is a better choice for multimedia performance and offers improved client performance, in most cases. However, client updates will need to be applied to each workstation, increasing the workload for maintenance and increasing the risk of software or hardware conflicts on each client. This can add substantial overhead to application support costs and work effort, depending on the number of workstations running the system.

Servers

A **server** is a high-end computer, or series of computers, that provides essential services across a network. Often they have a dedicated functionality, such as print servers, file servers, Web servers or database servers. Servers require a steady power supply and network connection. They tend to be noisy and generate heat while needing to remain a within a specified temperature range, which is why they are often housed in a dedicated room called a data center or server room. These rooms are equipped with a redundant power supply and control systems to monitor and moderate temperatures, humidity and other environmental factors.

When multiple servers are logically connected through a dedicated high-speed network connection, this is referred to as a cluster, and each server is referred to as a node on the cluster. This is used to provide server redundancy or load balancing wherein traffic is balanced between the two or more clustered servers, decreasing the workload of each.

In a hospital or hospital system, a server cluster may include many servers (nodes), which allows a portion of the cluster to be brought down without impacting the user's access. This is useful when applying software or upgrades or other maintenance.

In addition to easing software maintenance, distributing the workload across multiple servers expedites the computing processes and prioritizes tasks and scheduling or rescheduling them based on priority and user demand. Clustering also provides high-availability for the system. Each server within the cluster has the ability to take over for the other if necessary, due to failure of a node. Clustering servers can provide many benefits, but be aware that not all applications are cluster-aware or are able to utilize a clustered environment.

Storage Area Network

A **storage area network** (SAN) is a remote data storage device connected to servers that appears to be locally attached. A SAN typically has its own network connection that runs only between itself and the servers. System availability is further enhanced if the SAN has redundant storage to mitigate the risk of a SAN storage bank failure. The Fiber Channel fabric is a specially designed infrastructure to handle SAN communication. The access is much faster and more reliable than normal network protocols. This storage management solution provides increased flexibility, speed and scalability, but tends to be expensive.

Disaster Recovery

As is true of anyone leading an enterprise, project managers need to understand **disaster recovery**. This refers to how to recover your business from a disaster when the application, data or the entire system is made unavailable.

While full destruction of the data center can be considered a disaster, most often recovery is necessary when there are more localized problems, such as broken water pipes causing water damage, hardware failures or database corruption or a small fire. Disaster recovery includes everything from performing regularly scheduled backups to having disaster recovery standby sites. Each system should have a disaster recovery plan that outlines the activities to be taken in order to minimize the duration of loss of access. This plan should also include the acceptable recovery time and how this will be met if disaster occurs. The plan should be rehearsed at least once or twice a year to ensure it is realistic and achievable.

A **backup** is a duplicate, archive or copy of some or all of the files in a computer system to a separate location on the network or to some form of media, such as magnetic tape or CD. A full backup is the backup of all files and is often completed nightly, when usage is lower. An incremental backup is a procedure that only backs up files that have changed since the last backup. These can be scheduled at various times during the day and are less of a load on the performance of the system.

After a catastrophic failure of the system, data can be recovered by restoring the last full backup plus each incremental backup that followed in the order created. Any changes made to the system after the last incremental backup will be lost. The frequency of the incremental backups must be weighed against the impact of frequently scheduled backups on end user performance.

Disaster recovery sites are remote locations where impacted systems can be recovered. These are used to mitigate the risk of the current location becoming unusable. There are a variety of options depending on the acceptable recovery time. More critical systems may need to be recovered within four to six hours, while administrative systems may be able to wait 24 hours. A **cold site** is simply a location dedicated to this purpose. All hardware necessary for recovery must be procured, delivered and set-up before the recovery process can begin. Without this being done, the delay in recovery to a cold site can be substantial.

A better idea is a **warm site** which is set up with the necessary hardware that is close to matching what is in the current data center. The backups must be delivered, or made accessible, prior to restoring any system. Best of all is a **hot site**, which has all necessary hardware plus a near complete image of the current data with the systems waiting for the last backup of data to be restored. Hot sites are very expensive, but provide the quickest recovery of lost access. In any case, a cost-benefit analysis should be completed prior to choosing the type of recovery site. Also, it is important to understand that not all systems within the data center need to have the same disaster recovery strategy.

High Availability

High availability is a system design intended to achieve the highest level of availability possible for a system. More complex systems have more possible points of failure, which result in a higher risk. Redundancy provides a reliable alternative if something fails; an example is a backup power supply for power outages. The concept of redundancy can be applied to most components of any system, from the network to file storage.

As mentioned earlier in this chapter, clustered servers provide redundancy—if one fails, the work processes failover to the others in the cluster without impact to the end users. However, as with disaster recovery, redundancy can be expensive and should be considered based on a cost benefit analysis for the most critical systems.

Network

A **network** is a connection between multiple computers and other hardware, such as servers and printers, allowing them to communicate with each other and share resources. There are many options for network hardware from fiber optics, cellular,

Ethernet to wireless. The majority of hardware will be connected to the network through direct connection with an Ethernet cable. This is used for any computer or printer that will remain in a single location and provides a consistent connection. Ethernet is frequently deployed using other devices, such as hubs, switches or routers to join multiple smaller networks together.

With the introduction of electronic documentation comes the need to have computers that are located where patients are located. With most facilities, there is not room or the budget to put a computer at each bedside. Wireless workstations are one solution; they can be taken where needed. They were initially called **computers on wheels** (COW) and are now called **workstations on wheels** (WOW) because some found the term COW could be offensive if taken out of context. While WOWs can be taken anywhere, they can only access the network where a signal is available. A wireless network survey evaluates the current wireless network, if any, and provides guidance for where the access points should be placed to provide the best coverage with the least amount of dead zones, where no signal is available.

Interface

The term **interface** refers to the interaction between two components. This can be the interaction between an input device, such as a keyboard, with a processing device, such as a computer. An interface could also refer to the interaction between the user and a system, such as the screen design or **graphical user interface** (GUI).

This section will define the interface between two systems. For example, when a physician enters an order in the EHR for a specific lab order, the system would process the order and send a message to the interface, which then sends the message to the lab system. Once the specimen has been collected and processed by the lab, a second interface message would send the results of the test back to the EHR for the physician and nurse to review.

These messages are often processed through an interoperability standard called **Health Level 7** (HL7) developed by the Health Level Seven International organization, founded in 1987. HL7 provides a standard framework for the structure of the interface messages in which the data are stored in specific segments of the message.

Interfaces can be developed to process and send messages that are triggered by an event. In the example just given, placement of the order is the trigger. This is called a real-time interface, since the information is sent in real-time when the trigger occurs. The message would include a defined set of data. In the example of the lab order, the HL7 message might include data such as the patient's name, medical record number, date of birth, lab test(s) ordered and any special instructions. If translation is needed, such as when the source system has patient first name and last name, but the destination system is expecting patient full name, an interface engine is used to modify the data in the message between the two.

Another option for an interface is to schedule a message(s) for every so many hours or once daily. This is accomplished by developing a query to look for something specific, and if the criteria have been met, a message is sent to the destination system.

An example of this type of interface could be to run right before each meal a query to determine any changes in the patient's location since the last query. If there was a change, a message would be sent to the nutrition application with the updated location, so meals are delivered to the patient's current location at mealtime. This type of interface is sometimes referred to as a data feed, since it is feeding data at specific times of the day and is not triggered by a specific action.

When an interface is involved in a software implementation, it is very important to make sure the requirements are properly documented. This would include what data are to be sent and in what location or segment of the message. The format of the data being sent must also be defined. A mapping document is used to show how the data will appear in the message leaving the source system, if any manipulation will be done in an interface engine, and finally how the data will appear when the destination system receives the message. The technical staff supporting each system must approve these requirements to ensure they can work with the data as defined.

ENVIRONMENTS

When implementing software, it is rarely as easy as putting a CD in the drive and loading an application on your personal home computer. They are complicated and require time to design, develop and implement. Testing will need to occur, preferably before any training that is scheduled.

Often development, testing and training activities occur simultaneously, especially during normal operations and maintenance. How will each of these activities impact each other if they occur in the same environment, or instance of the system? Some say, "There is no test like production," but would you really want to use your live production system to do testing or training—probably not. In this section, the different environments will be reviewed. It is not necessary to have each of these for every software implementation, but a decision needs to be made early in the project planning phase regarding which ones will be utilized.

Sandbox

A **sandbox** environment is used for play. This is often used to experiment with changes when the impact is unclear. This is a stand-alone system that has limited extras, such as printing or interfaces. Only test data should be entered to verify the impact of any changes, and this environment should be refreshed periodically to clear out unwanted changes and test data. A sandbox is also used when developing software to provide a workspace to develop code in isolation, after which the changes are merged with other code.

Development

As the name states, this environment is used for **development**. The work completed in this environment should be approved through documented requirements and/or change requests. Once the changes are made, they are validated to ensure they were done correctly.

For example, if the list of allergy types is added to a drop-down menu through the use of a configuration tool, the developer should validate that the end user will see the list in the appropriate field and that the entries are in the expected order, either alphabetically or with the most common at the top. This is often a stand-alone system similar to sandbox and should only have test data entered. It is a good practice to refresh this environment with a copy of production once or twice a year to keep their configurations in synch. When this is done, the real patient data should be removed prior to use to ensure proper privacy controls.

Test

Once changes are verified in the development environment, they are moved to the **test** environment. This is where all the testing occurs and should be similar to production with test versions of any interfaces. These test interfaces should connect to the test environments of the other systems. This will allow full integration testing of the messages crossing between the two systems.

Test printers should be set up to verify any report or printing functionality. There are many ways to migrate the changes from development to this test environment. Tests can be refreshed with a fresh copy of development at regular intervals, or the changes can be unloaded and then loaded or they can be made manually.

Often the method chosen is directly related to the type of change and the options available within the system. For some smaller systems, the decision might be made to have a combined development and test environment. This provides the advantage of only keeping one environment in synch with production. The disadvantage is that testing is occurring while other changes are being made in the same system, which might invalidate the test results. The work effort for keeping extra environments in synch and migrating the changes should be weighed against the volume of changes and testing when deciding if separate environments are necessary or desired.

Pre-Production

Some testing requires an environment identical to production. **Pre-production** is a copy of production with all real data retained and having full functionality, such as interfaces and printing. A typical comment is, "There is no test like production."

Yes, production offers the best way to test exactly what end users will experience, but there is an element of risk when testing in production. However, pre-production provides this opportunity without risk. In this environment, however, the use of a smaller database and test data that might not be realistic can introduce limitations to testing. Having a full-size database also allows for performance and load testing. This environment does require a full copy of production, including hardware and interfaces.

Production

The **production** environment is where the end users actually do their work and use the system as it is intended. Real data that are entered continuously through direct data entry or via interfaces bringing information from other systems. This is the most important environment and must remain available and reliable for the users. As tested changes are migrated into this environment, the testing step is to validate that they were migrated correctly.

Training

There are a variety of ways to train end users in how to use the new system. If the training plan calls for any hands-on experience, a **training** environment should be considered. This is a static version of the system with defined training data that match the training materials. Generic training accounts are configured to provide specific access for the different classes of options. If the students will be entering data, the database should be refreshed regularly to clear out the extra information entered during the class. This allows each class to start at the same point.

When making a decision on which environments are right for the specific software being implemented, the project team needs to weigh the risks against the budget and available resources to support each throughout operations and maintenance. For smaller systems in which there will be minimal changes, a combined development and test environment along with production may be all that is needed. If the department using this small system has a very low turnover of staff, they might not need a training environment. When it is expected that there will be a need for ongoing training for new employees, such as for an EHR, a training environment might be necessary and desired.

Each environment needs to be maintained with updates, requested changes and hot fixes related to the system, database and even the operating system on the servers or workstations. This takes time and resources to complete, and needs to be repeated for each environment.

There is also the cost and maintenance of the hardware, network and storage for the databases. Some environments can be hosted on the same hardware, such as the development and test environments on the same server. This can save some cost for hardware, but updates that are related to the hardware or systems on the servers will be applied to all environments at the same time. This is one reason why production should always be on its own hardware. This physical separation allows testing of all changes prior to production implementation. The evaluation of options and final decision of how the system will be configured should occur during the project planning phase so the associated activities are scheduled, and each environment is ready and available when needed.

CASE STUDY 1
IMPLEMENTATION OF AN ELECTRONIC HEALTH RECORD (EHR)

Type: COTS

Additional Information

Your analysis of the current situation shows there are a few workstations in the nurse's stations with a single printer. No other workstations or printers are available except in offices.

The project scope includes multiple interfaces to and from the EHR. Patient demographic information along with ADT information will be sent from the EHR to the lab and radiology systems. Patient lab and radiology orders will also be sent to these two systems. Lab and radiology results will be sent back to the EHR.

It is expected that the physicians will enter their own orders utilizing the new CPOE functionality. The only other staff expected to enter orders would be nurses for phone orders only.

Questions

1. What environments would you anticipate you might need?
2. Would you anticipate the need for redundancy and disaster recovery for this system?
3. What might be some considerations when evaluating workstations and printers for the end users?

Feedback

Feedback for this case study can be found in the Appendix.

CASE STUDY 2
IMPLEMENTATION OF AN ORGANIZATIONAL
METRICS DASHBOARD

Type: Custom Development

Additional Information

Your analysis of the current situation shows that each of the users has access to a computer and printer. Most utilize a PC, while a few are using Mac workstations.

It is expected that each user will enter their own metrics data as they are gathered. Senior leadership would like to see the most current data in the dashboard whenever they log in.

Questions

1. What environments would you anticipate you might need?
2. Would you anticipate the need for redundancy and disaster recovery for this system?
3. What might be some considerations when evaluating workstations and printers for the end users?

Feedback

Feedback for this case study can be found in the Appendix.

CHAPTER 7

Software Testing

"Survey respondents estimated that if 100 percent of defects were addressed and remediated prior to production, they would experience a 32 percent cost savings."

—M. Ballou

Testing is one of the most important activities when implementing software of any type. This applies to the initial implementation, as well as the implementation of an upgrade or any change that is completed during operations and maintenance. In most software projects, there is a testing phase that occurs when all the development is completed and before training and the activation.

While this is an important phase of any implementation project, testing should actually occur throughout the project in one form or another. However, most of the test effort occurs after the requirements have been defined and the development has been completed. The software development methodology chosen leads into the definition of the testing methodology. The design needs to be carefully checked against requirements prior to any development to ensure that it meets the customer's needs and expectations.

Unit testing occurs during development to verify each piece of code or configuration prior to release to the test team. During the project planning phase, the test plan defines what type of testing will be completed, what materials will be developed, and the expectations of the test team. Expected deliverables from the testing phase include test scripts, test scenarios, test reports, test plans and how test incidents will be reported.

Tip

The National Institute of Standards and Technology and Research Triangle Survey (2002) reported that software bugs and errors cost the U.S. economy $59.5 billion annually. More than a third of this cost could be avoided by improving testing infrastructure.

Organizations that develop software or support software systems often have a specific person or team who focus on testing. Those doing testing need to understand the requirements and the new workflows for how the system will be used. They also need to be aware of the dataflows, or how data will flow through interfaces or within the system.

Tester training on how to use the system should occur during the project's early stages. The test team should review the requirements in detail to ensure they are all included in the testing process, either through detailed test scripts or broader scenarios. Testers also should meet with users to ensure that current workflow is addressed in final scenarios. These activities help the testers develop the scripts, scenarios and the expected outcomes for each.

There are a variety of testing types that are possible for software projects. How much testing and what types are needed for individual projects is highly dependent on the project itself and the amount of time available for testing. The organization's tolerance for risk and the defined risk mitigation strategies also will influence the plans for testing, as well as the organizational sensitivity and impact of the project.

A project related to pediatric medication dosing will have more stringent testing requirements than one related to scheduling. Both are very important to the organization and need to be done correctly, but one impacts patient safety while the other impacts patient and clinic inconvenience. Following are brief descriptions of different testing types and when they might be used in a software implementation project.

TESTING TYPES

Unit testing is the testing of individual software components to ensure they function as designed without generating unexpected errors prior to integration with other components. Generally, this testing is completed during the software's development and includes: checking the spelling of displayed items, ensuring they are in the correct location on the system screen and checking that data is saved as expected.

This concept applies to COTS systems in which the software is configured to meet the organization's processes. If, for example, there is an option of what happens when the user double clicks on a patient name in the patient list, does that actually happen when the configuration is complete?

Unit testing also is applicable for any ongoing changes made to the system once in operations and maintenance. This helps users verify that the configuration functions as designed without unexpected errors prior to being integrated with other components. Unit testing is also called "component testing" and is the only type of testing with which the developers should be involved.

Once development is complete, the code is moved to a dedicated test environment in which any changes are controlled to minimize the impact to ongoing testing processes. In this environment, **functional testing** is conducted to determine that the integrated components function as designed.

Functional testing is completed by testing staff and is based on functional requirements. Defined test scripts are used to perform functional testing; each script is written to verify a specific requirement or a group of requirements. Besides testing how the integrated components function as designed in the requirements, functional testing also ensures that the code follows the organizations business processes. This includes a series of tests using normal and erroneous data that should mimic what real users would enter.

Testing the integration or connection between multiple modules or portions of a single system is called **system integration testing**. This is used for testing the applied business process scenarios in conjunction with the components and interfaces to ensure that the system as a whole is functioning correctly.

This testing is based on business scenarios to demonstrate how systems work together. For example, if an order is entered for a chest x-ray, did the order cross the interface and does it appear in the radiology system? If expected, did the order requisition print in the radiology department or in the patient care unit? If you have a single sign-on solution and change your password, can you access each system with the new password?

System integration testing is full testing of the system with a focus on the big picture. This testing verifies that a system is integrated to any external or third-party systems defined in the system requirements. The test of a process, from beginning to end, is completed within scenarios rather than within detailed test scripts.

One example would be to admit a patient to the hospital and enter orders for a diet, medications, lab tests and oxygen therapy. Testing would include verifying whether the diet order went to the nutrition department as expected through an interface message or a requisition that prints. Did the lab system receive the orders for the lab tests? If results are entered, will they come back to the original system for the patient care staff to see? Are the medications and oxygen available for the nursing staff to document against? This testing is completed in the test environment or in the pre-production environment of each system being tested by the test team.

Once a system has been tested and modified, **regression testing** should be included in the test plan. If development is completed in phases, this would include the introduction of each additional phase.

Regression testing is a method of verifying that the new change does not break another part of the system's functionality. This should be completed on its own. Standard regression test scripts are documented to be followed each time a change is introduced and include a variety of basic features to ensure that the system functionality is preserved.

Similar in scope to a functional test, a regression test allows a consistent, repeatable validation of each component of the system after a new change. While regression testing can be performed manually, an automated tool is often used to reduce the time and resources needed to perform this repeatable testing.

When developing custom systems, it is important to test the system's compatibility with different workstation configurations. This includes different operating systems and hardware platforms. This type of testing is called **non-functional testing**. Are there specific minimum requirements for the amount of memory or size of the hard drive? Do the requirements define which browsers the system should work with? If not, this type of testing would help define the minimum requirements needed to run the system.

Vendors will provide the minimum requirements necessary for their systems when you purchase them. This testing is repeated as technology changes to verify that the system remains compatible with the latest versions and can be completed manually or through an automated tool.

Performance testing—also called load testing or stress testing—is completed in an environment that closely resembles production. This testing helps the technical staff in understanding the scalability of the system or in benchmarking the performance of new hardware. It is useful in the identification of any bottlenecks for high-use systems and is generally completed through the use of automated tools that can mimic peak-load conditions. It is also important to understand the accessibility of the system from the workstations located throughout the organization.

This would include understanding the performance of the wireless network. How many workstations will be located in a single location? What is the available bandwidth? Are there any dead zones in which the wireless network is unavailable, and is this acceptable?

User acceptance testing obtains confirmation by the business SMEs, preferably the owner or super user from the business community, on the usability and match of the software to mutually agreed requirements. This testing is scenario-based rather than technical.

One example of a scenario-based test is that of a new patient who has arrived on the hospital unit. The nurse performs his or her normal activities, but utilizes the new system rather than the organization's current paper-based process or legacy system. The test is scheduled and runs in a controlled environment, and the work is completed in the test or pre-production environments.

Be prepared to receive a lot of feedback from the users who are conducting this testing. This is likely the first time they have seen the system, and each will have opinions on improvements.

Every item should be noted, evaluated and categorized based on feedback or action items. Critical issues should be resolved before the end of the testing phase. Education issues should be provided to the training team to be incorporated in the training and possibly included in a FAQ document that can be reviewed by users prior to the activation. Some issues might need to be provided to the business owners for evaluation if they relate to the new workflows or processes. Categorizing the feedback will help the team focus on what needs to be resolved right away.

Parallel testing is similar to user acceptance testing, but the staff is doing their work using the current processes plus the new electronic process in parallel. This requires additional staff and is completed while in the work environment. When the patient arrives to be admitted, one admission clerk would admit the patient using the current paper process while another takes the same information and enters it into the new admission system. This provides more realistic evaluation of the business fit and workflows, but does require additional staffing and access to the system from the admissions department.

As mentioned earlier, the level of testing is dependent on the uniqueness, complexity and impact of the software being implemented. A small, simple system might only include a few types of testing, while the larger more complex systems would lend themselves to more.

There is no right or wrong answer on when to perform each test or whether some can be completed concurrently, such as combining function and integration testing.

CONFIGURATION MANAGEMENT

Configuration management is the discipline of controlling configuration items throughout the system's lifecycle. Configuration items are any single entity that can be uniquely identified. This includes portions of software code, hardware or documentation. Items can vary widely in complexity and size, ranging from a single software setting to an entire system.

Configuration management includes identifying, documenting, tracking, coordinating and controlling the current status of these items, their versions and relationships. The goal of configuration management is to ensure the integrity of the software and hardware. Strong configuration management imposes control over activities that are often unmanageable and complex.

The configuration management plan documents how this process will be integrated into an organization. The plan often includes definition of need, any policies or procedures, responsibilities and defined processes. It is important to identify what configuration items will be under configuration management, what information about the items will be tracked and what process a requested change goes through before being implemented into production.

Tools are available to assist with automating parts of the process and can provide a method of documenting the baseline of each configurable item, as well as provide version control when modifications are approved.

 Tip

Under configuration management, each change should be fully tested prior to migrating the change into the production environment.

All project managers are familiar with **change management**. The importance of managing changes to software and hardware is as important as managing changes with scope or requirements. The concepts are the same. This is a formal process to control and coordinate all changes to a production system. This process includes how changes are requested, prioritized and approved. A Change Control Board often undertakes these processes and includes key stakeholders, as well as IT SMEs. They have the authority to approve or deny requested changes based on evaluations and recommendations.

Once approved, each change should be fully tested and scheduled prior to being migrated to production. This should be a repeatable process that is fully documented and communicated. The decision on which environments are available for the specific system will define the steps of this process. Will there be separate development and test environments or one environment for both activities? See Chapter 6 for discussion on environments.

Release management refers to the activities surrounding the release of a specific version of the system. Changes should be introduced into an environment on a controlled schedule. This will reduce the impact to the users. Migrating changes to the test environment on a set schedule allows the testing staff to know exactly what needs to be tested and provides a stable location to test without constant changes that could impact the results. Packaging the changes into a scheduled release for production ensures they are migrated in a controlled manner. Only those that passed testing are included, and limits when changes occur that might impact the end users.

When implementing software, configuration management would begin as soon as a configurable item is identified and baseline information is collected. For software development, this would begin when a piece of code is completed and placed under version control. For a COTS implementation, this might be as soon as the configuration is complete.

In either case, configuration management begins prior to the main testing activities. Once the testing activities are completed, the system should be considered frozen until activation. This will ensure there is time to fully test all modifications and reduce the risk of last-minute changes having a negative impact on production.

CASE STUDY 1
IMPLEMENTATION OF AN ELECTRONIC HEALTH
RECORD (EHR)

Type: COTS

Additional Information

You have been informed that a group of super users has been identified to assist with the project. They are a combination of nurses and physicians who represent the different patient care areas. They have been involved in redesigning the workflows and developing the requirements for the order forms and documentation.

It took a long time to obtain agreement on how the clinical documentation will be developed and what terminology to use. The IT and vendor staff are now busy building the structured notes, flowsheets and free text notes.

The interface team has obtained approved requirements for each of the interfaces. The IT staff is busy working with the vendors from the EHR, lab and radiology systems to develop them.

Questions

1. How could you utilize the super users during testing?
2. What types of testing would you include with this project/program?
3. What types of items would be placed under configuration management?

Feedback

Feedback for this case study can be found in the Appendix.

CASE STUDY 2
IMPLEMENTATION OF AN ORGANIZATIONAL METRICS DASHBOARD

Type: Custom Development

Additional Information

You have been informed that a group of super users has been identified to assist with the project. They have been involved in developing the requirements for the new system and are familiar with all metrics collected.

Questions

1. How could you utilize the super users during testing?
2. What types of testing would you include with this project/program?
3. What types of items would be placed under configuration management?

Feedback

Feedback for this case study can be found in the Appendix.

CHAPTER 8

Activation Management

"If you always blame others for your mistakes, you will never improve."

—Joy Gumz

Planning for software activation begins during project initiation and continues through the Planning, Execution and Controlling process groups. Decisions made during these phases feed into the implementation strategy and how the software will be activated. With the project team's focus on system design, development and testing, true activation planning can be forgotten until it is too late.

This chapter will review what it takes to have a successful activation, beginning with initial planning through the post-live support of end users. Training also will be included, since this activity occurs right before the activation and is a key step to ensuring that the users are ready to begin using the new software when it is available. When the software is not ready or the users are unprepared, the initial perceptions will be negative and not easy to change.

 Tip

> There are a variety of definitions available for what activation planning means. For the purpose of this book, activation planning will be defined as the activities and planning surrounding the go-live or activation of a software system.

USER TRAINING

A training plan should be part of the project management plan, and it should outline how training will be accomplished and when. The size and scope of the project will define the type of training required. For the more complex project, the most common options are a trainer-led classroom, online computer-based training (CBT) or a combination of the two.

If a combination is used, one option would be to have the basic functionality included in the CBT, followed by classroom training that includes the more advanced features.

Having CBTs of a shorter duration allow users to complete them during their normal work hours. The training staff utilizes the requirements and design documentation to help plan what training materials will be required. The training should include the functionality of the new software, as well as any changes in workflow or processes to ensure that users are fully prepared for activation.

The quantity and type of courses will depend on the user population. Will different groups of users have access to different functionality? Do they need to be trained differently because of their security access? Will physicians, nurses and respiratory therapists all require the same level of training?

Understanding the different groups of users, what system functionality they will be using, and the level of security for the software will help make these decisions. Oftentimes, the development of the training material has to wait until the software is available to the training team. This typically follows the development or configuration phase of the project. Depending on the development strategy, they might have access to some functionality if it is being completed in phases or through an iterative process.

Training should occur as close to the activation date as possible, so the students do not forget what they learn. When there are 50 to 100 users, this might not be an issue, but when implementing an EHR with 3,000 users it can be more challenging.

The staff's normal work hours should be taken into consideration when scheduling training. Will classes be offered on the evening and night shift in a hospital setting? If training staff in a physician's practice, will the schedule be kept clear of appointments for training or will it occur after-hours?

Another consideration is whether the training will be mandatory. If it is, there needs to be consequences for those not attending, such as not receiving their access to the software until after they attend.

If there is a large group of people who need to be trained, one or more training rooms should be set up to allow the maximum number of students to be trained over the shortest period of time. However, it is important to keep classroom sizes small enough for optimal learning. Therefore, multiple classrooms might be needed.

In many cases, the workstations in the training rooms are provided with specific training patients and training logons. This allows students to have access to their own unique patient with the correct security access so they are learning with the same access they will have when the system is live. The patients will have specific data pre-loaded to coincide with the training materials. One example is when students are shown how to look up a patient's allergies; there should be allergies present for them to find.

Training is one of the key elements that can make the project successful. This is often the first time any of the users have seen the software, and first impressions tend to last a long time. Proper planning and execution is critical, along with the efforts of a dedicated training team. These activities coincide with planning for the actual activation activities; having a strong lead of the training team helps the project manager keep both activities on schedule.

ACTIVATION

Activation planning should begin as early as possible in the project's lifecycle. The larger and more complex the project, the sooner activation planning should begin. A general guide used by some is two to four months prior to activation for medium-sized projects and four to six months for large or complex projects.

Tip

> As a general rule of thumb, detailed activation planning should begin approximately two months prior to the activation for a smaller project. A larger, more complex, project could require four to six months.

Another factor that impacts the amount of activation planning required is the **activation strategy**. Will the users be moving from paper to electronic? Is there a legacy system into which the data will have to be migrated prior to the use of the new software? Will the new software be rolled out one area at a time? Will one area be a pilot, and if all goes well, will it be rolled out to all others at the same time? Answers to these questions will help you define the planning and activities needed to move forward.

Any decisions that were made early in the project should be considered when this planning begins. This will help identify remaining decisions. There are many decisions to be made and each will impact the activities to follow. The use of an **options document** will help compare each option to make an educated decision.

An options document includes a description of the decision to be made and a description of each option, along with various advantages, disadvantages and other key information, such as resources required and costs, all of which should be presented in a table to allow for easy comparison.

The team putting the document together also should provide a recommendation and justification for which option was chosen. While there seems to be a lot of information included, it is important to keep it simple and objective.

One major decision for any activation is the actual date and time of go-live. This might seem simple, but depending on the number of staff required for the actual activation tasks along with post-live support, it can be a real challenge.

Variables to consider include holidays, school calendars for children, scheduled vacations, historically high census periods and organizational activities, such as accreditation visits. The impact on end users also should be considered, especially when extra staffing is planned to help once the new system is live. Additional decisions would involve how to ensure the right data are available when needed.

If implementing an EHR, how will the patients, the active medical orders for the current inpatients or the schedules for the outpatients be entered so they are available when the users begin utilizing the system? What results will be entered? Will past lab or radiology results be loaded? If so, how far back? Some decisions are necessary early in the planning stage, while others will continue to be identified as planning continues.

As with project management, communication is one of the most important aspects of activation planning. This includes communication to all stakeholders, end users, organizational leadership and the project team. Once a decision is made on the date and time of the activation, this should be communicated so the departments can begin their preparations. Managers need time to schedule the appropriate staff, since clinical staff schedules are sometimes created six to eight weeks in advance.

As additional decisions are made and more information is gathered, you should have as your goal the kind of communication that arrives early and often and is clear and concise.

This can be challenging as staff may not always read their e-mails or remember what they read. A variety of communication methods should be used, such as flyers, posters and staff meetings. Be creative in getting the message out. Remember to also communicate any changes to these plans if the activation date or time slips.

Activation Checklist

Identification of the specific tasks that are required to activate the new software is an essential step to preparation. There are a variety of ways to identify and facilitate the documentation of these tasks, but this book will describe one—an **activation checklist**.

The checklist is a detailed list of all tasks that occur before, during and after go-live. It is similar to a work plan, but with more detail. The level of detail can be found all the way down to tasks with durations of only minutes. The development of the checklist begins with a face-to-face meeting of all staff involved.

During this meeting, detailed tasks are identified and then placed in sequence. An easy—and low-tech—way of accomplishing this is with the aid of sticky notes. (You could do this electronically, but many prefer the sticky notes because they tend to be a bit more interactive.) Each person at the meeting writes one task per sticky note and includes the resource and estimated duration. Once all tasks are collected, they are sorted by the order in which they should occur. These meetings provoke a lot of discussion, and a task identified by one person often triggers thoughts of others that should be included.

After this meeting, the tasks, durations, estimated start and finish times, resources and comments are entered into a spreadsheet. Remember to think of this checklist as a living document, something that will change each time it is reviewed and more information is obtained.

Regular meetings should be scheduled to review the checklist with the goal of having a complete list of all tasks. This **iterative process** helps to verify that the right tasks are identified, in the right order, with the right predecessors and assigned to the right resources.

Subsequent meetings often include some good discussion about what should happen, how and when. These are often important topics to get through, even if they appear to take the meeting off topic. (Some tasks can be completed concurrently, which will save time.) While the process is sometimes tedious, not having a checklist, or having an incomplete one, will lead to missing tasks or performing them out of order, requiring rework, frustration, extended downtime and unhappy users.

As the team reviews the checklist, they should be asked what could go wrong during each task. Discussing and planning for the worst will provide a strategy to be documented in advance, rather than trying to come up with a plan on the fly when the situation arises. This provides a level of **contingency planning**.

The contingency plan should include how to completely roll back to the previous version or system if the situation cannot be resolved. Some questions to ask: How would tasks be undone if needed? Where should go/no-go decisions go in the checklist?

Activation Rehearsal

Once the project manager and team feel the checklist is complete, the next step is a test by conducting an **activation rehearsal**. Running a full rehearsal of the activation plan will help validate the checklist related to tasks, their duration and order, as well as help to identify anything that is missing. This also provides a practice for any tasks that might be new to the technical staff. This should be as close to the actual activation as possible, and a copy of production should be used unless a pre-production environment is available.

For the rehearsal, as well as the activation, it is best if everyone is located in the same space to ensure proper communication and coordination. A person should be assigned to run the checklist, which means he or she coordinates what activities are happening, documenting any comments or changes being made, such as new tasks or any modification to the order.

Tip

It is not uncommon to hear an end user say, 'I didn't know about this.'

The project manager should be free to troubleshoot issues, communicate with others, and assist where needed. The task resources need to notify the checklist coordinator when they begin and end each task, as well as notify regarding any changes to the tasks themselves. This ensures that everything is correctly documented. Nothing should be deleted from the checklist; using strikethroughs and colored fonts helps to identify changes since the final checklist becomes a key document when preparing for the actual activation.

After the rehearsal, a lessons-learned meeting should be held. This meeting should be used to review the rehearsal event and review what changes are necessary for the real activation. The checklist is reviewed and modified based on the updates made during the rehearsal. This includes modifying the durations and order of tasks, as well as the tasks themselves.

Other lessons could involve communication, amount and type of staff needed, timing of when staff is needed and the overall duration of the activity, including the duration of any system downtime. The rehearsal is the time to make mistakes and, if it went very poorly or major modifications to the checklist were required, take the time to repeat the rehearsal prior to the actual activation.

Things to consider for the activation:

- Do you have a location large enough for all IT staff?
- Are there enough computers for all IT staff? Do they have laptops?
- Are there enough network ports, power outlets?
- Is there a phone available for a conference call for others to check in? Is it in a location at which everyone can hear and be heard?
- If some resources are remote, such as vendor staff, do they have the necessary access?
- Is there a way to display the checklist being updated, so all can see the most current version?
- Do you have a way to stay in contact with staff outside of the room?
- Do you need to provide food and drink for the staff? Is the cafeteria open during the activation? Will people have time to leave to get food?
- Do you have a mode of communication for users to request assistance? Is this needed during the downtime?

During the final weeks of activation planning, last minute fixes and training will be going on. It is important to institute a **system freeze** prior to the activation to ensure there is time to fully test all modifications and everyone can feel confident that the system is stable and ready for the activation. This should occur at least one week prior to go-live, but two weeks is better.

During these final weeks, communication will continue throughout the organization to ensure all are well informed about the upcoming activity. If there is a current electronic system that will be unavailable during the activation, the project manager should check to see if any hardcopy reports are necessary to support work processes or patient care during downtime.

All of the planning and preparations have led up to the day of the actual activation. The project team is aware of what is expected of them, when they need to be onsite, and what tasks they will be doing. The users know what to expect, whether there is a downtime or not. They have been trained and understand their new workflows and processes as well as the downtime processes.

However, despite all the work to refine and finalize the checklist and plan for any contingencies, something will come up that was not anticipated. Adding buffer tasks to the checklists, maybe in conjunction with the go/no-go decisions, will provide time to work past these unexpected surprises.

Building in plenty of time to complete system and regression testing prior to allowing users into the system will allow the team to resolve any issues that arose during the testing. With proper planning, the right people will be available, either in the room or by phone, to resolve any issues that come up.

Once the system is live, **post-live support** begins. This activity involves technical and clinical staff. Good planning is necessary for a smooth transition to the new software and work processes. Users will need help, whether it is in answering questions about how to do something or in resolving something wrong that needs fixing. Support staff should to be ready to respond when needed.

A Help Desk or hotline should be shared prior to the activation. Flyers posted on workstations also can help. Scheduling support staff should ensure they are available during business hours for a period of time after the activation. Users appreciate having the support staff making rounds and providing guidance and just-in-time training. (This should not take the place of having staff answering the hotline phone.) For some systems, this period of support need only be a few days, while larger implementations might require 24/7 support for weeks.

Users also will want to make modifications to the software; however, it is important that users become familiar with the software and the new processes prior to making any modifications. Of course, this does not include issues or patient safety concerns, which should be resolved right away. Users should understand the process of requesting future modifications, as well as how they are approved and prioritized.

Activation planning is a complex activity and includes several components. It requires a very detail-oriented person to help move the team through this lengthy process. With proper planning, the software will be successfully activated and the end users will be well prepared. Detailed documentation and clear, concise communication are two of the key elements of proper activation planning. Having all steps and configuration settings documented ahead of time ensures that the settings that were tested are the settings being implemented. This documentation also allows for other staff to step in and complete the task, if necessary. Remember, it is okay to make mistakes in the rehearsal as long as you learn from them for the activation.

CASE STUDY 1
IMPLEMENTATION OF AN ELECTRONIC HEALTH RECORD (EHR)

Type: COTS

Additional Information

The activation strategy decision is to go-live with all functionality in a Big Bang. This will include users in all inpatient care areas. The new production system will be configured, tested and ready when the code freeze on changes takes effect two weeks prior to the activation date.

All patients need to be loaded into the new system, along with their demographic information. It has been requested that the past two years of lab and radiology data be loaded into the new system. The manual entry of all active orders for the inpatients should be scheduled at the last minute.

Questions

1. What main activities would occur during the activation?
2. How would the activation change if this were an upgrade?
3. What level of post-live support should be scheduled?

Feedback

Feedback for this case study can be found in the Appendix.

CASE STUDY 2
IMPLEMENTATION OF AN ORGANIZATIONAL METRICS DASHBOARD

Type: Custom Development

Additional Information

The activation strategy decision is to go-live with all functionality in a Big Bang. This will include all users. The new production system will be developed, tested and ready when the code freeze on changes takes effect one week prior to the activation date.

It has been requested that the past year of metrics be loaded into the new system.

Questions

1. What main activities would occur during the activation?
2. How would the activation change if this were an upgrade?
3. What level of post-live support should be scheduled?

Feedback

Feedback for this case study can be found in the Appendix.

CHAPTER 9

Measuring Success

> "The question for the future is not 'What do you do?' or 'How do you do it?' but rather, 'What difference have you made?'"
>
> —*American Nurses Credentialing Center, 2010*

Measuring the success or outcome of a project can be viewed from two perspectives, both of which require attention at the time of project initiation. First, the **evaluation** of the implementation itself is essential to project managers, as the information obtained can be used as lessons learned for future projects. This perspective of the evaluation process includes determining whether or not the project met major milestones on time, whether there were budget overruns, whether key deliverables were implemented, whether resource allocation was appropriate and whether the final system met all defined requirements.

The second perspective of the evaluation process addresses whether or not the project met the overall business need and the reason the project was funded and supported by the organization. This chapter will briefly review the first perspective and then focus on the second perspective of the evaluation process.

Project success is often measured as being completed on time and on budget. While these are wonderful goals, they offer a narrow viewpoint and do not address whether the final deliverables were accepted by the customer.

Success factors around time and cost measure the project management methodology, but not necessarily all the activities of project or if the need was met. It is critical that the definition of criteria for success occur early in the project, as the project is being defined.

Project success factors can be derived from the documents developed in initiation and planning. Measuring whether the final software delivered matches the requirements that were approved at the beginning of the project, plus any approved changes would be one example.

 Tip

> The identified evaluation methodology should measure the quality and effectiveness of any software implementation.

If the plan includes migrating data from a legacy system, was it migrated successfully and in the expected format? Success factors also can come from any project constraints or assumptions. An example would be successfully utilizing the current hardware based on the assumption that no new hardware would be required. Project success factors should be measured by the time the project ends.

Each IT investment is undertaken for a reason. With significant financial investments in software, it is important to develop and implement a strategy to assess and confirm that the expected benefits are realized. Most of these evaluation activities will be completed outside of the implementation project.

Did the new CPOE system reduce medication errors? Did the new ADT system result in fewer duplicate patient records? Did the new electronic nursing documentation module result in more accurate clinical data? Did it reduce the amount of time nurses spend charting? Did the new system really make a difference?

This perspective of system evaluation looks at the organization's strategic objectives for undertaking the project. Some of these objectives might not be realized until months after the project officially ends, but a comprehensive evaluation is essential to ensure that the organization's time and money, both of which are significant, are well spent.

Clinical information systems are a major investment for healthcare organizations, not just in terms of dollars, but also in human resources. This significant expenditure for implementing, upgrading and enhancing these systems requires evaluation and justification.

It should be common sense that resources should go toward the implementation of safe and effective systems, but measuring this becomes difficult or is often ignored. With clear justification, organizations are beginning to demand outcome data from their investments in IT. The measurement of a system's success or effectiveness needs to be given consideration at the time of project planning.

Measuring outcomes from a system implementation is as variable as the projects themselves. The evaluation of each project is unique and based on multiple factors, including the organizational need, the desired outcome, and the data and resources available to perform the evaluation work.

A project's outcome may be measured in a number of areas:

Clinical Outcomes
- Reduction in episodes of ventilator-acquired pneumonia with the implementation of electronic order sets and/or appropriate reminders and alerts.
- Increased compliance with vaccinations or other routine examinations.

Financial Outcomes
- Reduction in or elimination of paper/toner.
- Reduction in duplicate processes/systems by centralization of systems.

Research Outcomes

- Improved accuracy of data to support research.
- Improved access to data by researchers.

Adoption

- Increased use of system or component by physicians.
- Increased use of system or component by nurses and other care providers.

User Satisfaction

- End user satisfaction level with new system.
- Usability of system is satisfactory.

Quality/Patient Safety

- Reduction in medication errors.
- Improved accuracy of data for clinical decision-making.

Administrative Outcomes

- Improved administrative report accuracy.
- Improved access to administrative data.

Productivity

- Reduction in time to document in new system.
- Workflow process streamlined.

From these examples, it becomes clear that a one-size-fits-all evaluation process to measure the outcome of an implementation project does not exist. It must be customized to fit the specific desire and expected outcomes. The plan can be derived from the documents developed in the initiation and planning phases.

It is at this point in the project that the organization's overall objective or outcome should be clarified. Oftentimes, the evaluation will require that **baseline data** be collected so that a comparison can be made at designated time intervals post go-live. This emphasizes the importance of investing time during the project's planning phase to think about and document how a project will be evaluated once the system is activated.

Project managers may not be involved in these measurements, as they are often conducted months or even years after the project ends. However, they should provide input into the process during the project and include any qualifiers that may impact the data collected pre- or post-activation.

For example, medication errors may appear to increase after the implementation of CPOE, and leadership might attribute this to a failed implementation. However, studies indicate that electronically collected data are more accurate than manually collected data; error rates are not actually higher with CPOE, just more accurate. Tracking trends over a period of time after CPOE will provide a better indication of the success of the implementation.

Determining what to measure can be a challenge. While **quantitative data** are typically preferred, the need for **qualitative data** is clear in the areas of user satisfaction and user experience with the new system. Along with the increased importance of evaluating outcomes, literature and industry tools for evaluation have appeared.

The Agency for Healthcare Research and Quality's (AHRQ) *Health Information Technology Evaluation Toolkit* (2009) is a valuable tool for determining what data to collect based on the project and desired outcome being measured.

In addition, the National Resource Center developed a compendium of health IT surveys that may meet the needs of a particular project's evaluation. Both the surveys and toolkit are available on AHRQ's Web site.

A thorough outcomes evaluation also should include a core set of **standard components** in areas such as the methodology, results, discussion and conclusion. There are a number of resources available to provide guidance and best practices for developing an evaluation plan to measure outcomes related to quality, rigor and applicability to the development of a customized plan. Other resources include several organizations that focus on healthcare quality; some are listed at the end of this chapter.

Tip

For each project, an organization should measure the success of the project itself and the success of meeting the need for which the project is intended.

Key to the success of an outcomes evaluation plan is the involvement of the business owners and senior stakeholders. Also, consider the involvement of the organization's central quality council, if one exists. These stakeholders are most familiar with the business need for the new system and can provide valuable input as the outcome objectives and the evaluation plan are developed. The **outcomes evaluation plan** should include:

- Expected outcomes or objectives.
- Operational definitions of each outcome.
- Points at which objectives are measured.
- Resources needed.
- Role of each resource defined.
- Determination of the need for baseline data.
- Data collection plan.

These details are defined in the plan, which should be approved by the project sponsors and are a key deliverable for the project. Any activities identified in the plan that occur during the project should be included in the project schedule. Once the project is complete, the work should continue according to the schedule in the **strategic metrics plan**.

When new software and workflow processes are introduced, there is a period of adjustment while the users are learning and understanding the changes. Any measurements taken during this time will be influenced by the learning curve, which will skew the outcomes. Depending on the size of the change, this may continue three, six or even 12 months after activation. Data evaluation should take this into account and the farther out from the activation, the better the trend should be.

Evaluating the system implementation should reflect the breadth of potential outcomes that can result. So many questions can be asked and evaluated. What are the attitudes of users toward the software, or even the new processes that came with the software? How well are they adapting to the new technology? What are patients' perceptions of the new processes? Do care providers spend the entire time with the patient looking at the computer? Do the patients perceive this as a distraction? What are the financial impacts of the new software? How long will it take to recover the cost of the implementation?

Simply measuring these outcomes is not enough; the data should be measured and decisions should be made based on the results. The goal is to continuously improve the quality, safety and user satisfaction, as well as to reduce costs. The key is to allocate the time and resources to evaluate the outcome of system implementation, starting in the planning phase.

Some organizations that focus on healthcare quality and safety include the following:

- The Joint Commission (www.jointcommission.org).
- Agency for Healthcare Research and Quality (www.ahrq.gov).
- The National Quality Forum (www.qualityforum.org).
- Institute for Healthcare Improvement (www.ihi.org).
- National Association for Healthcare Quality (www.nahq.org).
- American Health Quality Association (www.ahqa.org).
- Leapfrog Group (www.leapfroggroup.org).
- National Committee for Quality Assurance (www.ncqa.org).

CASE STUDY 1
IMPLEMENTATION OF AN ELECTRONIC HEALTH RECORD (EHR)

Type: COTS

Additional Information

Your activation was successful, and the end users are working through the expected workflow issues and trying to remember how to use the system. You have staff providing support, and this is much appreciated.

Questions

1. What metrics would you use to measure the success of the project?
2. What metrics would you use to measure the success of meeting the strategic objectives?

Feedback

Feedback for this case study can be found in the Appendix.

CASE STUDY 2
IMPLEMENTATION OF AN ORGANIZATIONAL
METRICS DASHBOARD

Type: Custom Development

Additional Information

Your activation was successful, and a few of the end users have entered metrics data. Others are not scheduled to collect and enter data for a few months. You had staff providing support, and it was appreciated. You have also provided a user's manual for those who might not use the system right away.

Questions

1. What metrics would you use to measure the success of the project?
2. What metrics would you use to measure the success of meeting the strategic objectives?

Feedback

Feedback for this case study can be found in the Appendix.

References and Additional Readings

Books

Aiello B, Sachs L. *Configuration Management Best Practices*. Boston: Addison Wesley; 2010.

Morris PW, Pinto JK. eds. *The Wiley Guide to Project, Program & Portfolio Management*. Hoboken, NJ: John Wiley & Sons Inc; 2007.

Project Management Institute. *A Guide to the Project Management Body of Knowledge*. (*PMBOK®*) 4th ed. Newtown Square, PA: Project Management Institute; 2008.

Project Management Institute. *The Standard for Portfolio Management*. 2nd ed. Newtown Square, PA: Project Management Institute; 2008.

Schach SR. *Classical and Object-Oriented Software Engineering with UML and C++*. 4th ed. Boston: The McGraw-Hill Companies, Inc; 1999.

Schiesser R. *IT Systems Management*. 2nd ed. Boston: Prentice Hall; 2010.

Schwalbe K. *Information Technology Project Management*. Cambridge, MA: Course Technology; 2000.

Web sites

Agency for Healthcare Research and Quality (www.ahrq.gov)

American Health Quality Association (www.ahqa.org)

American Nurses Credentialing Center (www.nursecredentialing.org)

American Nurses Credentialing Center, Magnet Recognition Program (www.nursecredentialing.org/Magnet.aspx)

American Nursing Informatics Association and Capital Area Roundtable on Informatics in Nursing (www.ania-caring.org)

American Medical Informatics Association (www.amia.org)

Association for Configuration and Data management (www.acdm.org)

Healthcare Information and Management Systems Society (www.himss.org)

HIMSS Project Management Special Interest Group (www.himss.org/ASP/sigs_project.asp)

Institute for Healthcare Improvement (www.ihi.org)

The Joint Commission (www.jointcommission.org)

Leapfrog Group (www.leapfroggroup.org)

National Association for Healthcare Quality (www.nahq.org)

National Committee for Quality Assurance (www.ncqa.org)

The National Quality Forum (www.qualityforum.org)

Project Management Institute (www.pmi.org)

Software and Systems Engineering Vocabulary (http://pascal.computer.org/sev_display/index.action)

Appendix: Case Study Feedback

DISCUSSIONS FOR CASE STUDIES

This final section provides feedback for the case study questions presented at the end of each chapter. You were only provided minimal information about the two case studies prior to being asked the questions. If you were actually managing these projects/programs, however, you would have considerably more information at hand to make decisions. Further, it is important to note that some decisions are based on the culture of the organization rather than best practices, so please remember there are no right or wrong answers.

CHAPTER 2

Case Study 1: Implementation of an Electronic Health Record (EHR)

Type: COTS

Included Functionality

- Allow management and tracking of patient demographics along with ADT information.
- Provide CPOE.
- Allow results retrieval (i.e., interfaces from lab and radiology information systems).
- Provide clinical documentation for nursing, including eMAR.

Current Situation

Your organization has just purchased an EHR system from a well-known vendor. You have been assigned to implement this system. Upon review, you learn that the current system used for patient demographics and ADT will be replaced with the new EHR. Your laboratory and radiology departments have information systems in which they manually enter the ordered exams and subsequent results. The results are provided to the patient care areas on paper to be placed in the hard copy medical record. All clinical documentation is completed in the paper medical record and is unstructured.

Questions

1. Would this implementation be managed as a project or a program? While this could be managed as a project, it would be best managed as a program. This implementation is very large and would benefit from being broken down into separate projects with someone managing the day-to-day work for each.

2. If managed as a program, how would you break it down into separate related projects? There are a variety of ways to separate this program into individual related projects. The following is a list of potential projects:

   - ADT processes: This includes working with the admissions department to ensure their workflows and processes are evaluated and updated with the new system.
   - Order entry: This includes evaluation and configuration of all possible orders, related order forms, the method of viewing the patient orders, how they will be completed, etc.
   - Clinical documentation: This includes the process of gaining consensus on terminology and standards for documentation, along with the configuration of the actual document templates, flowsheet templates, the eMAR, the method of viewing documentation once entered and any signature management processes.
   - Results retrieval: This includes configuration of how results will be viewed. Will there be an option to filter, sort, trend, etc.?
   - Interfaces: This includes analysis and development of all interfaces.
   - Technical implementation: This includes all work around installing and configuring the entire system, including hardware, software, databases, clients, selected environments, etc.
   - Reports: This includes the work processes surrounding the configuration of reports, either viewable reports or printed reports.
   - Testing: This includes the entire testing processes once the configuration is complete.
   - Training: This includes all work efforts around end user training, from development of materials, coordination of space, scheduling and actual training.
   - Activation planning: This includes all work surrounding planning for the activation and post-live support. If desired, the post-live support could be broken down into a separate project.

Case Study 2: Implementation of an Organizational Metrics Dashboard

Type: Custom Development

Included Functionality

- Allow online data entry for defined metrics by staff doing data collection.
- Provide high-level dashboard views of metrics results for executive leadership.
- Provide ability to drill-down into details of any metric in dashboard.

Current Situation

You have been asked to develop software to replace the multiple spreadsheets currently in use to track operational metrics. Upon review of the current situation, you find that the metrics data are currently being collected into separate spreadsheets. The spreadsheets are consolidated and provided to the executive leadership of the organization on a monthly basis. The metrics include a variety of items, such as patient wait times, returns to the operating room, post-procedure infections and quantity of medical and nursing students.

Questions

1. Would this implementation be managed as a project or a program? This is an appropriate size to manage as a project.
2. If managed as a program, how would you break it up into separate related projects? Not applicable because of the option chosen.

CHAPTER 3

Case Study 1: Implementation of an Electronic Health Record (EHR)

Type: COTS

Additional Information

The vendor offers a full suite of functionality and modules for the hospital, which includes a standard interface for lab and radiology, but your organization has not developed these interfaces before. The nurses use a paper medication administration form, but clinical documentation is free text without any standard structure. Physicians use order forms for writing patient medical orders that are processed by unit staff with copies sent to the necessary departments.

Questions

1. What types of training might be included in the training plan for this project/program? The training plan might include the following classes:
   - Introduction: Provides basic navigation processes. For example, looking up a patient, finding results or documentation. This class would be useful for all users, even for those who will have *view-only* access.
   - Order entry: Provides education on how to enter orders. This class would be useful for physicians, as well as for nurses who potentially might enter phone orders.
   - Clinical documentation: Provides education on how to document through all options, such as flowsheets, notes and the eMAR. This class would be useful for nurses.

   Another option would be to have a class for physicians and a class for nurses that cover all the functionality each would use. These classes could be in addition to an introduction course. You could also provide a separate course for non-physician and non-nurse staff.
2. What might be some challenges faced by the project/program team? This program will have a very large program team. The main challenges will focus around communication and coordination. It will be very difficult to get the entire program team to attend any single meeting or series of meetings. It will be easier for the individual project teams to meet regularly.

The program management team, program manager and the project managers must meet regularly to ensure proper communication and collaboration across the entire program.

Also, project managers will need to be accountable for communication to their project team regarding program-related information that will impact the team's work. If possible, it would be beneficial to have regularly scheduled program meetings—every other month or quarterly—for as many people as possible. During these meetings, the status of individual projects, new risks, key issues and key decisions can be shared. This will also allow a forum in which questions may be asked.

3. What roles or skill sets would be required for the project/program team? The following is a list of roles that might be required for this program. Depending on the work effort required, and how much time the staff has to dedicate to the program, multiple people may be needed within each role.
    - Program sponsor(s)
    - Program manager(s)
    - Systems administrators
    - Network administrators
    - Database administrators
    - Application administrators/configuration
    - Business analysts/workflow analysis
    - Report developer
    - Interface developer
    - Testers
    - Trainers
    - Help Desk/support staff

Case Study 2: Implementation of an Organizational Metrics Dashboard

Type: Custom Development

Additional Information

There are a limited number of people, approximately 15, who collect the metrics data on a set schedule. The frequency of the different measurements varies from weekly to annually. The system should be able to allow data entry and data storage for each frequency. One goal identified early is for the new system to be Web-based for easy access.

Questions

1. What types of training might be included in the training plan for this project/ program? With the limited number of users for this new system, training might include a demo to all, along with a user manual for reference. Another option would be to have super users provide one-on-one training to the users regarding how to enter their metric data. The latter might be a better option if the different metrics have different workflows within the new system.

2. What might be some challenges faced by the project/program team? The challenges for this project are related to obtaining good requirements and controlling the scope. When the owners cannot see something to say they like or don't like, or cannot see specific functionality, it is hard to gather all requirements. They often do not verbalize everything they have in their minds as to expected functionality or the way they want the system to look and feel. This is the reason why more development models include a prototype or follow an iterative process. The challenge is to control how many iteration steps will be included, so they do not go on forever.

3. What roles or skill sets would be required for the project/program team? The following is a list of roles that might be required for this project. Depending on the work effort required, and how much time the staff has to dedicate to the program, multiple people might be needed within each role. Also on some projects, one person might be able to fill multiple roles. For example, the application developer might also serve as the report developer; the business analyst might also serve as the tester or trainer. This would depend on their skill set and availability.

- Project sponsor(s)
- Project manager(s)
- Business analyst/requirements
- Application developer
- Report developer
- Systems administrator
- Database administrator
- Testers
- Trainers

CHAPTER 4

Case Study 1: Implementation of an Electronic Health Record (EHR)

Type: COTS

Additional Information

The vendor provides a standard work breakdown structure (WBS) plan that outlines a 16-month implementation plan. The new hardware has been ordered. They have assigned the following resources:

- A project manager to manage vendor work and resources.
- A trainer to provide training for project team and super users.
- A clinical consultant to facilitate workflow redesign.
- A configuration consultant to provide guidance and assistance for system build and customization.
- A technical specialist to provide guidance and assistance for the technical configuration related to hardware and database.
- A technical interface specialist to provide guidance and assistance for the interface development.

Questions

1. What types of requirements are needed for this project/program? The contracting documentation should have a list of all requirements the organization was looking for related to what they purchased. For the program tasks, there are a number of requirements that need to be defined and approved. The vendor is providing a system with a lot of functionality, but your organization might not choose to implement all of it due to its implementation strategy or because it does not offer the service that fits with the features. During the project-planning phase, a decision should be made regarding what functionality will be implemented and what will not. This should be part of the scope document and should be managed as part of the scope. Additional requirements would include the following:

   - Reports: This includes what reports the users will view or print, what information will be included, and how will they look. It is wise to include the medical records department if any reports will become part of the permanent medical record.
   - Interfaces: This includes the requirements regarding what information is to be included in each interface, the flow of the data, what manipulation is necessary and where will it be done, and the location of each data element within the Health Level 7 (HL7) message.
   - Clinical documentation: This includes what terminology will be used and exactly what will be built. The importance of gaining consensus across the entire organization on how the documentation will be done cannot be understated. With that said, this should be fully documented and approved before any configuration is completed.

   Changes to all requirements should be controlled through a change management process similar to the scope management process.

2. What types of line items would you expect to find on the budget? The budget for this program could include:

   - Software licenses from vendor.
   - Software licenses for any third-party applications necessary for vendor's software to function (i.e., database licenses).
   - Hardware, including servers and workstations.
   - Professional services from vendor for their staff to assist with implementation.
   - Contract staff, if your organization requires supplemental staffing for this program.
   - Training for the project team, which might be offered onsite, online or at the vendor's location.

3. Who would you expect to be stakeholders for this project/program? The stakeholders would include the entire program team, all physicians, all nurses, all other users of the system: medical records, radiology, and lab departments; admissions and the organization's leadership.

4. What methods of communication might the project manager utilize for this project/program? The project manager could use any number of the following methods of communication. This is not an exhaustive list, so be creative when communicating on any project or program.
    - Meeting minutes
    - Town hall meetings
    - Steering or governance committees
    - Department staff meetings
    - Flyers
    - E-mail
    - Newsletters
    - Booth/table near cafeteria
    - Web site

Case Study 2: Implementation of an Organizational Metrics Dashboard

Type: Custom Development

Additional Information

The project sponsor has identified three key people with whom the team should work to define requirements. They will be the super users who can also assist with testing. An experienced developer from the IT department will build the new system. He will utilize a platform that has been used for other custom applications and it can be hosted on current servers in the data center.

Questions

1. What types of requirements are needed for this project/program? This project should include business requirements that define each metric, the data collected, including the format, and the details around what is expected for dashboard view. The design requirements might be separate or may be combined with the business requirements. Any requested reports also should be defined in the requirements.
2. What types of line items would you expect to find on the budget? The budget for this program could include the following items:
    - Software licenses for platform used for development.
    - Software licenses for any third-party applications necessary for software to function (i.e., database licenses).
    - Hardware, including servers, if necessary.
    - Contract staff, if your organization requires supplemental staffing for this project.
3. Who would you expect to be stakeholders for this project/program? The stakeholders for this project include the project team, the staff who collect the metrics, the organization leadership who will view the dashboard and anyone else involved in the workflow or data flow.

4. What methods of communication might the project manager utilize for this project/program? The project manager could use any number of the following methods of communication. This is not an exhaustive list, so please be creative when communicating on any project
    - Meeting minutes
    - E-mail
    - Stakeholder meetings
    - Web site

CHAPTER 5

Case Study 1: Implementation of an Electronic Health Record (EHR)

Type: COTS

Additional Information

The vendor has provided details about how the new system can be customized. The organization can decide and build the following:

- Forms used for physician orders.
- How orders are displayed once entered.
- Format used for clinical documentation.
- How clinical documentation is displayed once entered.
- How results will be displayed when posted from the interfaces.
- How medication orders will be posted for documentation on the eMAR.
- Reports that are displayed and printed from the system.

Question

1. What phases would this project/program include? This program would probably include the following phases, which are more general. Depending on the decision about how to break the program into projects, some projects might not include all of these phases.
    - Program initiation.
    - Program planning.
    - Workflow analysis and redesign (may be part of planning).
    - Requirements definition (may be part of planning).
    - Program team training.
    - Technical system set-up and configuration.
    - Application configuration (to include reports).
    - Interface development.
    - System testing.
    - End user training.
    - Activation.
    - Post-live support.

Case Study 2: Implementation of an Organizational Metrics Dashboard

Type: Custom Development

Additional Information

The following functionality is being requested:
1. Allow direct data entry for 10 specific metrics collected throughout the organization.
2. Provide the ability to load the past two years' worth of data.
3. Provide dashboard views of data, with the ability to click on any value to view more detailed data.

Question

1. What phases would this project/program include? This project would probably include the following phases, which are more general. Depending on the development strategy decision, some projects might not include all of these phases.
   - Project initiation.
   - Project planning.
   - Requirements definition (may be part of planning).
   - Application development following the development strategy.
   - System testing.
   - End-user training.
   - Activation.
   - Post-live support.

CHAPTER 6

Case Study 1: Implementation of an Electronic Health Record (EHR)

Type: COTS

Additional Information

Your analysis of the current situation shows there are a few workstations in the nurse's stations with a single printer. No other workstations or printers are available except in offices.

The project scope includes multiple interfaces to and from the EHR. Patient demographic information along with ADT information will be sent from the EHR to the lab and radiology systems. Patient lab and radiology orders will also be sent to these two systems. Lab and radiology results will be sent back to the EHR.

It is expected that the physicians will enter their own orders utilizing the new computerized practitioner order entry (CPOE) functionality. The only other staff expected to enter orders would be nurses for phone orders only.

Questions

1. What environments would you anticipate you might need? Based on the size of the work effort and the need for strict control over any changes, the following environments might be chosen:

    *   A sandbox to provide a place to configure new functionality when it is unclear whether it will fit or be used.
    *   Development for all configuration development.
    *   Test: To separate the test environment so any additional configuration does not impact the testing of the system.
    *   Training: This will require a large training effort, and the system used should be isolated and should match the training materials.
    *   Pre-production: If you have the hardware, this would provide a good method to test right before going to production without impacting the end users.
    *   Production.

2. Would you anticipate the need for redundancy and disaster recovery for this system? Most definitely. This is a critical system for patient care and should be configured with full redundancy and to allow a quick recovery in the event of disaster. This would include an offsite location for recovery when the data center has the disaster.

3. What might be some considerations when evaluating workstations and printers for the end users? When evaluating workstations, it is important to understand where the users will be when they need access. For patient care, this is often at the patient's bedside, in the medication room and at the nurse's station. For others, access will be needed in the admissions department, in medical records, in various ancillary departments such as radiology and lab, as well as in some private offices. Access might be required in physician offices and in various other locations throughout the organization or offsite.

    With each of these locations, the physical space, along with network and power availability, needs to be evaluated. If there is not room for a full workstation, consider a workstation on wheels (WOW) as an option or maybe a laptop or tablet for portability. With these options comes the need for reliable wireless networking.

    When evaluating printers, the location, physical space, network and power availability also apply. The analysis of what printing will occur should feed into the quantity needed. Is it the expectation that this is an electronic system and that minimal to no printing will be done? Will all order requisitions, documentation, and results print in all patient care areas and be put into a paper medical record? The type of printing should also be evaluated, such as the printing of labels, reports and wristbands, which may require different printers.

Case Study 2: Implementation of an Organizational Metrics Dashboard

Type: Custom Development

Additional Information

Your analysis of the current situation shows that each of the users has access to a computer and printer. Most utilize a PC, while a few are using Mac workstations.

It is expected that each user will enter their own metrics data as they are gathered. Senior leadership would like to see the most current data in the dashboard whenever they log in.

Questions

1. What environments would you anticipate you might need?
    - Sandbox or development: Multiple sandbox environments to provide a workspace for each developer, if there are multiple developers. In the case of only one developer, the development environment would work.
    - Test or pre-production: To separate the test environment so any additional development does not impact the testing of the system.
    - Training could occur in the test/pre-production environment, since there are a limited number of users, and the system should not require ongoing training. This is dependent on the training strategy.
    - Production.
2. Would you anticipate the need for redundancy and disaster recovery for this system? This is not a critical system, but some redundancy would be beneficial for power and the network if there are concerns over stability. The organization leadership will want to have access when needed and avoid any perception that the system goes down frequently. The disaster recovery plan would include backups of the data for restoration as needed. This would probably be a lower priority for recovery if a disaster strikes.
3. What might be some considerations when evaluating workstations and printers for the end users? It appears all users have access to a workstation. This new system should be built so it is compatible with PC and Mac workstations. If the new system is Web-based, verifying that it works with multiple browsers should be part of the test plan.

CHAPTER 7

Case Study 1: Implementation of an Electronic Health Record (EHR)

Type: COTS

Additional Information

You have been informed that a group of super users has been identified to assist with the project. They are a combination of nurses and physicians who represent the different patient care areas. They have been involved in redesigning the workflows and developing the requirements for the order forms and documentation.

It took a long time to obtain agreement on how the clinical documentation will be developed and what terminology will be used. The IT and vendor staff are now busy building the structured notes, flowsheets and free text notes.

The interface team has obtained approved requirements for each of the interfaces. The IT staff is busy working with the vendors from the EHR, lab and radiology systems to develop them.

Questions

1. How could you utilize the super-users during testing? The super-users could be involved in identifying the scenarios that feed the test scripts. They could be involved in user acceptance testing, if this is part of the test plan. Depending on their skill set, they could be brought in to assist the test team with integration or system testing.

2. What types of testing would you include with this project/program? For a program of this size, unit testing, functional testing, integration testing, system testing, performance testing and user-acceptance testing would all be appropriate. Regression testing will occur after the main test phase, if any modifications or fixes are made, as well as any post-live changes.

3. What types of items would be placed under configuration management? Configuration management should be in place for the hardware configuration and software configuration, including modifications, updates and full upgrades. Items that change frequently, such as user accounts, registered workstations and printers, do not need to be controlled through a configuration management process.

Case Study 2: Implementation of an Organizational Metrics Dashboard

Type: Custom Development

Additional Information

You have been informed that a group of super users has been identified to assist with the project. They have been involved in developing the requirements for the new system and are familiar with all metrics collected.

Questions

1. How could you utilize the super users during testing? The super users could be involved in providing test data for each of the metrics and assisting with the testing of how the data are loaded. They could be involved in user acceptance testing, if it is part of the test plan. This might not be necessary if they are actively involved in other testing.

2. What types of testing would you include with this project/program? For a program of this size, unit testing, functional testing and system testing would all be appropriate. Regression testing will occur after the main test phase, if any modifications or fixes are made, as well as any post-live changes.

3. What types of items would be placed under configuration management? Configuration management should be in place for the software code to include any modifications. Items that change frequently, such as user accounts, do not need to be controlled through a configuration management process.

CHAPTER 8

Case Study 1: Implementation of an Electronic Health Record (EHR)

Type: COTS

Additional Information

The activation strategy decision is to go-live with all functionality in a Big Bang. This will include users in all inpatient care areas. The new production system will be configured, tested and ready when the code freeze on changes takes effect two weeks prior to the activation date.

All patients need to be loaded into the new system, along with their demographic information. It has been requested that the past two years of lab and radiology data be loaded into the new system. The manual entry of all active orders for the inpatients should be scheduled at the last minute.

Questions

1. What main activities would occur during the activation? The main activities includes:

Pre-activation date

- Communication.
- Final set up and configuration of production environment.
- Migration of all configurations to the production environment and validation that it was migrated correctly.
- Data loads of patients and results up to a specific date.
- Adding of interface threads to production—the result interfaces could be turned on for all new results starting at the specific end date for file load.
- Load of all user accounts—once this is complete, all new user accounts should be added as each request is received.
- Turn on all system backups, if not completed before.
- Meeting with support staff to provide a hand-off.

Activation date

- Enter all active orders for current inpatients into production system.
- Turn off current ADT system.
- Final load of patient data with any changes since end date on above file load.
- Turn on production interfaces, if not completed before.
- Activate all reports.
- Validate new system prior to turning it over to end users.

2. How would the activation change if this were an upgrade? The main change would be that the system is completely down and unavailable during the upgrade activities. This would require a documented downtime process for the workflow when the EHR is unavailable. Typically, activities include preventing the users from accessing the system and turning all interfaces off to prevent any changes to the system. The vendor would provide guidance on the upgrade steps that are necessary. If any configuration is necessary for new functionality, it will be completed after the system is upgraded. Then the system and modifications would require validation to ensure all changes were correctly made. Once interfaces are turned on, there is no turning back, since this will cause a change to the database. The go/no-go decision should be made right before the interfaces are turned on.

3. What level of post-live support should be scheduled? This is a major change for the users, and it will impact most of the organization. It is recommended that onsite support be provided 24/7 for a few weeks at least. Schedule for longer than you expect, since it is easier to cancel support staff for the evening and night shifts then to try and schedule them at the last minute based on need. Having staff making rounds through the areas using the new system provides just-in-time training and puts a face to support; both are welcomed by the users. There should also be a method for the users to call when they need help and no one is around.

Case Study 2: Implementation of an Organizational Metrics Dashboard

Type: Custom Development

Additional Information

The activation strategy decision is to go-live with all functionality in a Big Bang. This will include all users. The new production system will be developed, tested and ready when the code freeze on changes takes effect one week prior to the activation date.

It has been requested that the past year of metrics be loaded into the new system.

Questions

1. What main activities would occur during the activation? The main activities would include the following:

Pre-activation date

- Communication.
- Final set-up and configuration of production environment.
- Migration of all code to the production environment and validation that it was migrated correctly.
- Data loads of metrics data for past years.
- Set-up of user accounts.
- Turn on all system backups, if not completed before.
- Meeting with support staff to provide a hand-off.

Activation date

- If all was prepared ahead of time, the users can just start using the system.
2. How would the activation change if this were an upgrade? The main change would be that the system would be unavailable during the upgrade activities. Since this is not a critical system, communication should go out to the users regarding when the system will be unavailable. Once the upgraded code is migrated to production, it should be validated to ensure all changes were correctly made before users are notified that it is available.
3. What level of post-live support should be scheduled? Providing a method of communicating to the support team should be a sufficient level of support. Scheduling a super user to be with users when they first enter their metrics data would provide some just in time training if necessary based on how user-friendly the system is.

CHAPTER 9

Case Study 1: Implementation of an Electronic Health Record (EHR)

Type: COTS

Additional Information

Your activation was successful and the end users are working through the expected workflow issues and trying to remember how to use the system. You have staff providing support, and this is much appreciated.

Questions

1. What metrics would you use to measure the success of the project? The project can be measured by any number of criteria. Here is a list of some, but the list is not all-inclusive:
   - All patient-related ADT and demographic data were successfully migrated to the new EHR.
   - All patient lab and radiology data for the past two years have been successfully loaded and are available to the end users.
   - The system configuration matches the requirements. This can be split to be specific to orders, results or clinical documentation criteria.
   - The interfaces are live, match the requirements and pass the expected data between systems in the expected format.
   - The project was completed on time and on budget.
   - The hardware arrived on time and was set-up and configured according to the plan.
   - All end users attended training and received accounts, although it is hard to measure how well they understand the training.
   - The activation was completed within the defined timeframe.

2. What metrics would you use to measure the success of meeting the strategic objectives? The strategic objectives for this project could have included a reduction of errors, reduction of duplication of work, improved access to the patient information, and improved accuracy of data for patient care decisions. With this in mind, the following could be measured, although this is not an all-inclusive list. It is important to have a specific target in place for each metric. When applicable, each metric should include a defined target so the organization knows when they have met their objectives.

    *   Reduction of medication errors.
    *   CPOE for medication orders.
    *   CPOE for non-medication orders.
    *   Reduction of printer paper usage.
    *   Reduction of time spent documenting.
    *   Increased accuracy of heights and weights in the system.
    *   Increased completion of mandatory documentation (i.e., restraints).
    *   Increased accuracy of medication charting.
    *   User satisfaction surveys.

Case Study 2: Implementation of an Organizational Metrics Dashboard

Type: Custom Development

Additional Information

Your activation was successful, and a few of the end users have entered metrics data. Others are not scheduled to collect and enter data for a few months. You had staff providing support, and it was appreciated. You have also provided a user's manual for those who might not use the system right away.

Questions

1. What metrics would you use to measure the success of the project? The project can be measured by any number of criteria. Here is a list of some, although it is not all-inclusive.

    *   All metric data for the past two years have been successfully loaded and are available to the end users.
    *   The system developed matches the requirements. This can be split into the data entry requirements and the dashboard requirements, if desired.
    *   The project was completed on time and on budget.
    *   No additional hardware was required for the project.
    *   All end users attended training and received accounts, although it is hard to measure how well they understand the training.
    *   The activation was completed within the defined timeframe.

2. What metrics would you use to measure the success of meeting the strategic objectives? The strategic objectives for this project could have included an improved method to view and evaluate the ongoing metrics for the organization.

These metrics probably feed into organization decisions for patient care and operations. With this in mind, the following could be measured, although is not an all-inclusive list.

- Increased efficiency and productivity of staff gathering and assembling data, as measured by number of hours spent before and after the use of the new system.
- User satisfaction of users gathering and entering data.
- User satisfaction of organization leadership in relation to access to data in a usable format.

Index